A HANDBOOK OF PARISH STEWARDSHIP

OTHER MOWBRAY PARISH HANDBOOKS

A handbook
of
PARISH
STEWARDSHIP

Gratitude and Generosity

by
GORDON STRUTT
**An Assistant Bishop in the
Diocese of Canterbury**

**MOWBRAY
LONDON & OXFORD**

Copyright © Gordon Strutt 1985

ISBN 0 264 67018 3

First published 1985
by A. R. Mowbray & Co. Ltd
Saint Thomas House, Becket Street, Oxford, OX1 1SJ

Printed in Great Britain by
Billing & Sons Ltd, Worcester

British Library Cataloguing in Publication Data

Strutt, Gordon
    A handbook of parish stewardship : gratitude
    and generosity.
    1. Church of England—Finance 2. Christian
    giving
    I. Title
    254.8   BV772

    ISBN 0-264-67018-3

Contents

Foreword

I am happy to commend this handbook of Christian stewardship to the Church for study and use. Bishop Gordon Strutt has been closely involved in matters concerning the resources of the parishes in manpower and money for over a quarter of a century, and it is good that his particular approach has been preserved in the handbook.

I hope that it may be widely used by clergy and lay people to present the challenge to a firmer commitment which is the key to an adequate discipline about Christian giving and community service.

Expectant faith believes that God will supply what is needed in any way he chooses, and not least through the self-giving of his people.

+ROBERT CANTUAR

Introduction

Many have asked why the fact of stewardship and its concern about the gospel, personality and money has come so much to the fore in Christian thinking over the last two decades or so in this country. When shoes pinch it is time to get a new pair. Much as we might wish it were otherwise, it was because the financial shoes began to pinch that successful experiments in a new approach to church finance in other parts of the world were tried out in England.

The Wells Organization was the pioneer in what at that early stage was the raising of church income from the incomes of church people, and the techniques of capital fund-raising were employed very successfully on the basis of a three year pledge with a promise of no other requests for money. Some of the ideas which were basic to this form of fund-raising and the methods employed brought out problems of a theological nature which forced theologians to examine the whole project critically and in depth.

Books were produced, mainly in North America, by theologians in Lutheran, Methodist, Anglican and other Churches which looked at stewardship from the Christian as well as the human point of view and began to apply the great doctrinal themes of creation and redemption. As a result of this, Christian stewardship emerged as a challenge to the Church which not only affected its collection and use of money, but recalled it to a new responsibility for the gospel and the care of neighbour. Unfortunately, some of the profound insights of this new thinking were imprisoned in slogans such as 'money, time and talents' and the 'need of the giver to give' which were not always understood in the widest possible context. Many local churches were afraid of talking about money and wrapped an unpleasant topic in the cotton wool of time and talents. Experience in teaching Christian stewardship brought a balance between promotion and project which gave due place to personal response in committal to Christ. This began to expect a responsible view of all money and a new realism in giving a proportion of income for the work of God and for general benevolence.

The motivation moved from the physical need of the building or of the institutional Church to a recognition of the call of Christ to all his followers to be involved in his work not only by prayer but by gift and service.

The Church of England recognized the increasing importance of a proper understanding of stewardship and produced the famous 'blue book' entitled *The Christian Stewardship of Money*.

After a representative conference at which this book was launched, a central advisory committee was set up under the direction of the late Canon Hodd (later Archdeacon of Blackburn). Canon Hodd saw his task as a temporary one with the object of setting up an organization in every diocese to propagate Christian teaching on stewardship and to offer help in the conduct of stewardship campaigns. At about this time a northern business man put his financial resources behind the launching of an English company to offer professional and competent advice and help in the promotion and conduct of stewardship campaigns. Planned Giving Ltd, soon made a significant contribution in promoting and conducting a great number of initial campaigns. Generously, but perhaps unwisely, it shared its experience and an insight into its techniques with a gathering of diocesan advisers at Swanwick.

Many dioceses had set up a diocesan stewardship office with a layman in charge, having the task of promoting, conducting and following up stewardship projects and campaigns. Other dioceses appointed a clergyman to provide this kind of help in stewardship on a part-time basis, drawing his salary from the care of a parish. The amount of teaching and the degree of its theological content varied widely over the country. Some men were finding it impossible to cover the three departments of their work with equal vigour and efficiency. Others had to withdraw from time-consuming and adequate direction in order to supervise a large number of efforts by parishes entered into on a 'do it yourself' basis. In some, money for God was bedevilled by the demands of the institutions for survival. Release can only come when gifts of money and offers of service are seen as a measure of response to the love of God demonstrated first in the coming of Christ as man and, secondly, in the self giving of Christ through the Cross.

Any giving which condescends to help God do his work, or is in repayment of a debt owed to the Almighty, springs from conceited and heretical thinking. The theology which deals with creation, redemption and present and future kingdom, knows nothing that detracts from the sovereignty of God or that replaces the dependence of the human race upon God for life and sustenance. The dominion of man in the natural sphere may appear to be limitless, but it is a delegated dominion. Man is free and unfettered in his exercise of authority and his exploration of his environment, but there is an ultimate with which he must reckon as surely as he reckons with his own mortality.

Stewardship, which so often begins for a man in the challenge to him to look at his wealth with new and Christian insights, is concerned with the place of man in the universe, the responsibility which is his as a user and conserver of natural resources, as well as his responsibility as a manipulator of these resources or an inventor of new processes which may or may not be beneficent. Stewardship is a powerful word from God to all men, whether they be Christian or not, warning them of the danger and responsibility in the use and deployment of the forces of personality, wealth and power over others. The Church has received and acknowledged the demonstration in Christ of a life which was utterly God centred and responsible. What Christ can mean to the Christian can be made plain by a life lived by the same principles of responsibility and stewardship.

In conversation at conferences and in parishes it is discovered that there are clergy who feel that this teaching which arises from a faith in Christ which demands commitment, is beyond the understanding of the man and woman in the pew. They are thought only to be capable of seeing stewardship as a new and profitable way of solving parochial and diocesan budget problems. Questions put to laymen and women produce answers in some cases which cast doubt on the ability of the clergy to teach these truths. But parishes which had planned carefully to put themselves on a stewardship footing in all dealings with money and Christian responsibility have not regretted the effort nor the continuing demand for watchfulness and application. Where professional help in a campaign had been sought it was well founded and the response in terms of money well above the national average and greatly encouraging to the development of the work. Efforts conducted cheaply without competent guidance were generally disappointing to those engaged in them and low in their standard of giving. Proper teaching ought to have a spiritual effect as well as providing increased income.

Is it possible to uncover the causes of resistance to the acceptance of stewardship principles in the conduct of parish affairs? The benefits reported in so many parishes are obvious in terms of willing helpers and adequate annual incomes. Perhaps the causes are psychological. Some find a secure retreat in a declaration of acceptance of stewardship but a dislike of campaigns.

Many of the mistakes in terminology (all is not stewardship which is thus termed) and technique of the past have been discovered and abandoned. The fear of failure is more difficult to combat and this is found in some clergy upon whom, in great loneliness, the whole weight and burden of a church's life and finance has fallen. He carries so much, anything more might lead to breakdown and failure. Yet stewardship offers the opportunity for sharing the load, for getting the lay people involved in their proper task as having a part in ministry as they are part of the people of God. The clergy teach the truth of stewardship, train their people to think and to be articulate about their faith—the people in their turn, using what expert guidance is available, tackle a worthwhile job in a Christian stewardship project.

In other instances, parson and people together refuse to embark on any scheme which would offer more people the opportunity to give for the right reasons, because they say they have enough money and can always raise it without difficulty. They too have fallen into the error of supposing that stewardship is fund-raising.

In preparing the material for this handbook I wrote to all the diocesan bishops asking for information about the management of stewardship affairs in their dioceses. I am most grateful to stewardship chairmen and advisers through whom the answers have reached me. There is a notable air of keenness and commitment to the task among those who are giving so much time and effort to establish good stewardship, but there is also evidence of feelings of frustration in the face of much apathy and prejudice. It is my hope that this book may assist incumbents and parochial church councils in their pursuit of a well based understanding of stewardship. Group study of the biblical material will stimulate discussion and make it possible for everyone to grasp what may have been a large and rather forbidding subject. I hope that my fellow clergy may find some help here as well, as they prepare their sermons.

I have said elsewhere that our approach to stewardship has to be flexible and this may be a disappointment to those who look for a blueprint of method such as would satisfy any parish at every stage of its development. Mulling over ideas, discussion of possibilities and assessment of the real situation will lead to worthwhile results.

There is still a great deal of work to be done to make clear that the Christian stewardship of money is not simple, or complicated, fund-raising. Fund-raising is a respectable operation in a once-for-all drive to meet a deadline, to deal with an emergency or to tackle a capital project, but its ethos is quite different from the Christian's stewardship of his income. By a right attitude to income he can show his committal to Christ and his desire to serve him by generous and sacrificial giving of a proportion of the whole (for which God has to be thanked) for God's special work and for general benevolence. In this connection the biblical tenth has a twentieth century interpretation as part of a continuous response when it is taken as a starting point for prayer, thought and decision.

Perhaps the greatest scandal is that parishes which refuse to embrace stewardship are content to accept the benefits in a diocese and deanery which come from the greatly increased quota payments of stewardship parishes. An electoral roll and average communicant attendance may be much alike in two similar parishes but one pays £1,000 a year and the other very much less. Even when a diocese opts for some basis of quota assessment related to potential, where fair shares are expected from every parish, there are problems about the acceptance of an imposed figure and sometimes this leaves room for very little joy or cheerfulness in giving. If stewardship teaching were universally accepted, one of the results would be equality of sacrifice, and another a buoyant economy which would allow for many more good neighbour, evangelistic and overseas projects to be undertaken.

Canterbury
October 1984

GORDON STRUTT
An Assistant Bishop in the Diocese of Canterbury

Chapter 1

Historical Background

'Why this burst of interest in stewardship?'

'Haven't you heard? The squire has died.'

For too long too many have been dependent upon too few and it has been difficult to analyse the variety of motives which get people involved in church maintenance and kingdom extension. The habit of the squirearchy in England in their dying years 'to pick up the tab' as a matter of duty, effectively relieved the majority of worshippers from any feeling of responsibility or of having any say in the work of the local church. Legislation to give the people a representation at all levels of church life went a long way to correct this isolation of the people in the pew. The first shock wave was felt when the squire died; no longer a generous fount of largesse to meet the bills; no longer an assurance that repairs would be carried out and deterioration halted. Nevertheless there remained a complacent and ignorant confidence that the parson gets a good stipend.

To apathy comes a slowly awakening awareness that the death of the squire is not the only disaster to overtake the church housekeeping. Fuel is getting expensive, food costs more, wages must go up, the frosty fingers of inflation begin to shrink limited resources and more money is needed just to keep the ship afloat. Parochial church councils begin to become involved with church treasurers agonizing over the disparity between income and expenses. Cuts are considered, as a consequence of which missions and charities enter their period of shortage and anxiety.

In the late 1950s news reached England about the ways other parts of the Anglican Communion had set about rationalizing their finances. In many ways the English Church seems to have a built-in myopia which prevents it seeing what goes on in other parts of the world. A blindness and a self satisfaction which combine to prevent thought, experiment and the employment of new ways of working.

New Thinking

In 1910 the Bishops in South Africa put out a pastoral letter on church finance to the clergy and faithful laity. They recalled a principle that 'all wealth is a trust from God to be used for him. All members of the Church should therefore make an annual budget to guide them in their personal expenditure. First and foremost should each one of us set aside a definite proportion of our income for the maintenance and extension of the work of the Church of which we are members.' Here was an attempt to recall their people to a proper view of the source of all wealth and the accompanying responsibility for its handling and its distribution. About the same time financial stress in the Church of England prompted the Archbishops of Canterbury and York to respond to comments in the Lambeth Conference Report of 1908 by setting up a committee on church finance. That part of the findings of that committee which stressed what we now recognize as the principles of stewardship lost impact in the resultant flurry of activities which set up the organization of boards of finance which has served the Church so well since the report began to be implemented in 1911. This was the result of the first Lambeth reference to the stewardship of the Church's resources.

Impetus was given to the subject in Lambeth 1958 when the bishops offered a definition of stewardship as 'the regarding of ourselves—our time, our talents and our money—as a trust from God to be utilized in his service', and then went on to say, 'a parish without a sense of stewardship has within it the seeds of decay'. In 1978 the bishops concluded that the paucity of resources arose, not from a universal poverty, but from a wrong attitude of Christians to their possessions. The breakthrough into generosity, expansion and general usefulness would not come from any mysterious centre but from the combined commitment of individuals. 'We claim that God has already given his people all the human and financial resources necessary to carry out his mission in the world' (Page 101, Lambeth Conference Report 1978).

Missionary Call

It was early in this century that Vedanayagam Samuel Azariah showed his outstanding intelligence and breadth of vision by taking the lead with others to accept the clear demands of the gospel that Christ's followers should all become involved in missionary work. Indians began to move from the passive role of sheep in the European missionaries' flocks, to become shepherds themselves. By this means they would show gratitude to their white 'parents in Christ' and demonstrate their own ability to obey the missionary call with their own money and their own men. This urge towards independence and self sufficiency remained with Azariah well into his episcopacy as the first Indian Bishop of Dornakal, to which area he had first gone as a missionary himself. But missionaries need a firm base, and Azariah gave a lot of thought to the problem of the local church's own support. Western missionaries had turned their Indian converts into a 'receiving Church' and with that attitude Azariah discerned the acceptance of the hopelessness of poverty, a situation in many cases far from the truth. He began his programme of stewardship with some very practical teaching. It started with the women being asked to put aside from their cooking a handful for God. The accumulation of these handfuls could be sold for a respectable sum, and such a stewardship exercise caught the imagination of the practical Indian mind. In 1939 he wrote *Christian Giving* in Tamil; it was later translated into Telugu, and in 1954 it was published in the World Christian Books series in English.

Right Principles

In the 1950s when Christian stewardship was beginning to demand attention at all levels in the Church of England, Azariah's book proved a great source of stimulation. He was emphatic that right basic teaching was all important and discerned, what many an Anglican later discovered for himself, that even right teaching has a hard struggle to drive out wrong ideas which have taken hold. Giving for self support can serve a kind of selfishness and pride which has nothing to do with giving motivated by love of Christ. Only selfless generous giving can become a source of spiritual power.

Azariah was a devoted Bible student and in his book pleads for a biblical foundation for the principles which should control Christian giving. Money is important but it must not receive a total emphasis. Biblical teaching could never accept a motive for giving which is inadequate, unworthy or ineffective. There are spiritual lessons to be learned from the biblical view of our human and Christian responsibilities and these must be looked at in our chapter on the subject of the biblical foundation of Christian stewardship. Although the subject of Bishop Azariah's book is specifically Christian giving, he never confuses the spiritual exercise of generous support with haphazard fund-raising as a means of continuing to exist as a church. No one would disagree that fund-raising is a perfectly legitimate exercise in an emergency or as support for a secular project but

> giving within the Christian community for God and
> his kingdom must be an expression of the stewardship
> of individual and corporate resources.

In America

In the early 1950s the Episcopal Church in the United States of America settled for an annual visitation of church members which was called the 'every member canvass', when each was asked for a promised contribution regularly for the ensuing twelve months, to enable the local church to face the demands of its budget. The motivation tended to be the response to the

needs of the church as an institution and there was no built-in
opportunity for church members to see the challenge as a
spiritual one. Too often the level of giving was regulated by the
level of need and the average pledge in two similar areas would
differ widely on this account. Occasionally the teaching got
things in the right order and gave the opportunity for self
assessment which meant a release of generosity relating to the
spiritual state of love for God, rather than a share in keeping
things going. Bishop Emerich of Michigan, USA, tells a story
which unveils the error of finance-orientated thinking on the
part of a church member, who approached his church treasurer
with a question, 'Well, how much do you want me to give to the
church this year?' The treasurer was a man who practised and
taught tithing and was not greatly impressed. He replied, 'We
don't want your money', and walked away. Mystified by a
treasurer who refused money, the Easter churchman caught up
with him and said, 'Why don't you want my money?' The reply
came, 'We don't want your money, we want you. Worship God
every Sunday in this church for two months and then I'll talk
with you about what you should give.' No doubt others were
weaned from a superficial annual contribution in response to
the canvass to an understanding of the deepest meaning of
stewardship.

Before the dawn of the 1960s the professional help used in the
every member canvass in America came to this country in the
shape of the Wells Organization, which with the freshness of an
American approach and with no inhibitions about money
introduced a high powered fund-raising campaign for Christian
churches in their pursuit of an adequate expression of their
stewardship. Many were critical of the 'secular' tone of the
Wells approach, but as the famous blue book puts it '... if
English church people need to be taught the principles of
Christian stewardship—as they do—and if the Church in this
land lacks men trained to teach this subject—as it does—we
should be sufficiently humble to accept the help which the fund-
raising companies offer' (*The Christian Stewardship of
Money*, CIO 1959).

Early campaigns in England

Planned Giving Ltd was set up by a churchman in Manchester, Sir Kenneth Boardman, to provide an anglicized version of the Wells approach and to plough back into the dioceses a proportion of the profits. Meanwhile, at Church House, Westminster, Canon Norman Hodd dedicated himself to the training and establishment of stewardship experts in every diocese. In those early days the pattern of early campaigns included a parish dinner, an intensive visitation of a large contact roll, after the discovery of energetic laymen who could give a weighty financial lead.

From 1958 onwards large parishes were involving themselves in projects for improving their finances and some paid little regard to the theological foundations of Christian stewardship, and the degeneration towards simple fund-raising began and has continued. Others, from the motive of saving money, set about doing campaigns themselves and very soon corners were being cut, promised contributions were lost without trace in a welter of secrecy. Sausage rolls and coffee provided by the long serving women's groups replaced the dignified parish meal.

Most campaigns depended upon a renewed effort every three years and those visitors who had worked so hard in the initial effort were expected to begin again; but some had suffered unhappy experiences in their visits because of the emphasis on the collection of subscriptions for the church. The movement began to run out of steam and it was clear that there must be a search for a simple theological understanding of stewardship that would leave money in its important place. This would mean a return to the thoughts of those who had spoken and written about stewardship at home, abroad, and in successive Lambeths. Some latched on to a setting for the jewel of stewardship in a combination of time and talents. There was nothing wrong with that if time and talents were to express the devotion of the individual's existence and achievements to the glory of God. But the organizers' desire for specific analysis led away from the overall picture into a series of limited possibilities in the use of time and the exercise of talents. Often without research into local needs, offers of help were solicited from parishioners which could cover a list as long as forty activities. Not only were some offers never taken up, but the ludicrous situation could arise when ten people could offer to read to the blind when there were no needy blind in the parish.

An examination of stewardship activity in other parts of the Anglican Communion reveals attempts to include much more teaching in projects.

The teaching by preaching from the pulpit, by lecture and study group would begin some time before the actual start of a campaign. This had the effect of dealing with criticism and answering serious questions so that the ground was cleared for the intensive phase of the project. Earlier these questions had arisen during the short, sharp, concentrated few weeks of special effort with a lasting divisive effect because they could not be dealt with reasonably and at leisure.

In Australia

In the Anglican diocese of Perth, Australia, stewardship and training come under the umbrella of the Board of Education. Before a stewardship programme is launched there is often a six months' preliminary course of training of the laity undertaken by the Christian Education Group, and another period of training is available at the conclusion of the campaign turning the minds of Christian people to the ongoing commitment to mission. Clergy have expressed disappointment that the Perth scheme does not lend itself to a pastoral care scheme in which they can involve the laity. It seems to be a matter of policy that there should be a simple concentration upon the commitment in terms of money, with a net cast wide over families in the parish with even the slightest connection with the church. This leaves the way open for those who never come to church to have some part in giving, and offers a programme which gives no offence to committed people.

There is no stewardship department in the diocese of Sydney but this does not mean that Christian giving is at a low ebb. Committed Christians have absorbed teaching about the tithe over many years and they think in these terms so that shortage of money is not a problem where there is a tithe-based response. Large denomination dollar notes are common. However, some parishes in an endeavour to put their budget and finances on a firm base have used the services of professional organizations, but the ongoing work does depend upon the hard work of a few lay people. Occasionally the three-year programme has been transformed into an annual canvass of every member. In a province with very little endowment, there is a realism about responsibility for maintenance and expansion, and Sydney moved courageously into a scheme for a new Church House on ten floors which cost A$22 million to complete.

The diocese of Brisbane contains the headquarters of Compton Associates, a company which gives help and advice in two fields. First, that of fund-raising for community projects and secondly Christian stewardship in any of the Christian denominations. In 1976 a visitor from England discovered that, true to the aphorism that 'a prophet is not without honour save in his own country', very little help was sought from Compton's by the diocese, but that the Methodist Department of Promotion from Sydney was regularly employed. Literature used indicates the thinking behind any appeal for money, which puts a firm challenge to the faith of the churchman.

'Parishioners will be challenged to make a commitment based on the depth of their faith and not on the needs of the church.'

In the diocese of Melbourne all diocesan stewardship work has been committed to a specially formed private company called Church Advisory Services. There is a managing director and several campaign directors. They receive salaries at the same rate as the clergy in the diocese together with expenses and allowances for a house. This helps the team spirit when there is involvement with a parish campaign. The company charge fees with the object of keeping afloat rather than making a profit. They have worked out a variation on the three year plan having a special effort every other year. Three months before the intensive fourteen day period of the campaign, the incumbent

and the vestry are put in the picture. After the intensive phase
visitors are used for quarterly visits to those who have made
promises and belong to the scheme. A contract with the
company obliges the signatories to work together for four
years. It is reckoned that such serious co-operation means that
the impetus created will be maintained. Reports indicate
enthusiasm for an arrangement which treats the Church
Advisory Services as a handmaid of the church and produces
results beyond the provision of funds, in improvement in
congregations and in the numbers of adults coming forward for
confirmation.

In New Zealand

It was in New Zealand where the impact of Compton
Associates was most apparent. In the unique situation of
Anglican dioceses there the first essential was seen to be the
unequivocal lead given by the bishop. The involvement of a
whole diocese requires tact as well as strong leadership and a
project well grounded in the theological principles, expressed
by thankfulness to God for his goodness and a determination to
accept the responsibility of caring for other people in the name
of Christ. In a small country the making of community based
on a caring congregation proved an easier task than in the
conurbations of the United States and Great Britain. Nevertheless, the demand for understanding of principles and for a
vision of what might be, was no less pressing here than
elsewhere. Of course there are difficulties about a diocesan-
wide effort; despite all the prayer and teaching and despite a
strong episcopal lead there will be those, clergy and laity, who
will stand aloof. In the diocese of Nelson's first incursion into a
corporate effort three parishes refused to join in, two others
were lukewarm and never got off the ground. It is from the non-
co-operative background that talk of failure emerges. All
deaneries have since been involved, in turn, producing teaching
material for use in the quarterly pastoral visitation.

The most encouraging phenomenon of work in Nelson has
been the build-up of care for those linked with the church. The

number of families to be catered for is limited to five for each pastoral visitor. This limitation prevents superficial hurried calls but does require a large number of visitors. An ongoing exercise is the recruiting of more visitors, mainly through those already doing and enjoying this work. In New Zealand over seventy per cent of the population live in suburbs or towns and this percentage will increase. The stewardship of the church's manpower and resources must present a challenge that goes beyond finding money to keep the church going. The warm fellowship of Christ's people has to be offered to the lonely and unfulfilled folk who live in the neighbourhood. The Christian steward responds by investing himself in the friendly approach which leads to open-hearted talking and, above all, listening. For the New Zealander stewardship points beyond the mere conservation of resources, beyond the expression of fellowship which is a warm glow or a firm handshake, to a sharing of what is valued most. Here the evangelistic note can be heard as knowledge of Christ is shared through simple witness to what is beyond price. Once the visitor is seen to be a key person, not only in the stewardship project but also in the parish, more care and thought are given to a training programme for visitors, making them more proficient in that work, but also giving them a firmer grasp of the essentials of the Christian faith and enabling them to articulate their personal witness to the love and care of God in Christ.

Changing Methods

As time has gone by methods of conducting stewardship campaigns have been overhauled, refined and improved in efficiency, but the underlying principles once discovered remain the same. Once the challenge to devotion has been acknowledged then the giving becomes a matter of finding the best way to do it in the local circumstances. The best way ought to include the possibility of a personal act of giving—a banker's order would take care of the transfer of money but physical presence at a service of worship with the actual donation of an envelope establishes an act of offering which could be described as sacramental.

The maintenance of the Church and the support of other missionary activity has come a long way in the last four centuries. Endowment with money and land to pay the priest and repair the church had been developing from the eleventh century. Early tithing was a voluntary matter but by the time of the Tudors it had been incorporated in the country's tax system with non-payment penalties which included excommunication. In due course a church rate emerged which enabled church-wardens to pay for fabric repair; but that as well as the tithe as a compulsory imposition passed into history. The emphasis on voluntary support caused the introduction of cash collections at services, alongside the money given as alms at the service of Holy Communion. Church expenses became a regular fund to receive the congregations' offerings, to be supplemented by 'holy trading' at the church bazaar and some chance benefit by the low priced gamble, which worried some thoughtful people as giving little honour to God whose promise to supply all needs seemed to be overlooked. However, the voluntary principle was well established and soon the administrators wisely took a hand with 'freewill offering' schemes, one of which provided support for mission work by the provision of two envelopes for each Sunday.

Then the squire died. Budgets of expenditure exceeded income and people began, for all the wrong reasons, to talk about stewardship.

Chapter 2

Biblical Foundation

All stewardship arises out of a relationship. Between the owner
and his manager, the landlord and his tenant, the mistress and
her maid and the king and his chief minister, there are bonds of
responsibility. The book of Genesis unveils God the creator as
the owner of all that is. Adam, his dependent creature, is given a
place and authority as the caretaker gardener who will watch
over creation and exercise a limited dominion. There will be
room for the exercise of his own wisdom and initiative. In Cain
and Abel we see the division of responsibility. One cares for the
land, the other for the animals. Soon it is clear that something
has gone wrong, not in nature but in the human spirit. In
pictorial language the damage is described and is seen to be an
inflation of the self in wilfulness and cupidity. The steward
abandons loyalty, disobedience turns bliss into struggle. A
fundamental principle of stewardship, which should assure
peace and well-being to the household, is lost in the words of
Cain, 'Am I supposed to take care of my brother?' (Gen. 4.9.)

There are those who would wish to confine stewardship to a
religious context, identifying the ideal Christian with the
responsible steward. All human beings, even those who do not
possess the special graces and gifts of the spirit which derive
from Jesus Christ, are responsible within their environment to
care for it and for their own species. To avoid taking a proper
place, accommodating the needs of others, caring about the
tract of country designated 'my place', or to become simply

selfish in living with no regard for people, flora, fauna or the soil of his inheritance, may be a denial of responsibility but it does not banish it. Everyman is supposed to take care of his brother and within the wisdom of the Jews and their scriptures and the acts and sayings of Jesus this fact is made abundantly clear as part of the creator's plan.

Abraham's steward

Abraham had a servant, to whom he had given charge of his affairs trusting him to act wisely and shrewdly on his master's behalf. Given a general outline of what Abraham wanted as a wife for his son, Eliezer was left to the exercise of his own initiative. He was a man of prayer and, of course, that helped. He did not congratulate himself when he perceived that his mission had been successful but bowed his head and worshipped the Lord who had led him to his master's relatives. It is important for our study of stewardship to notice the characteristics of this man Eliezer. The relationship demanded and received trustworthiness in the servant; in fact they trusted each other. He had been given special responsibility, for he had charge of all that Abraham possessed. He was able to operate 'with a free hand' within the limits of the task. He was expected to give an account, even if the mission had not been successful. In this case success meant an accession of joy to Abraham and a blessing for his son Isaac and his wife Rebekah. The true steward brings happiness to himself in the exercise of his responsibility and to those around him who become involved in the outcome of his service; though dependent, he can act independently. Being one of God's stewards is not to live in a straitjacket.

Failure in stewardship

There is an interesting story amongst the oracles of Isaiah. In Chapter 22 there is condemnation of a certain steward Shebna who had been false to his trust and had used his authority to benefit himself. The prophet is commanded to challenge Shebna over his misuse of his stewardship and to pronounce a judgement on him as a shame of his master's house. He will lose his stewardship and the status which goes with it.

But note, from verse 20 onwards, another is called to be steward, one Eliakim who will assume authority and be a father to the house of Judah. He will bear the keys, he will be fastened like a peg in a sure place. But stewardship is no easy option, his very success by bearing too many burdens and doing it all himself puts too much strain on that peg and it gives way. Perhaps he learned the lesson and, when delivered from the burden, was free to act profitably for himself and for Jerusalem and Judah.

Stewards in charge

In the Old Testament the concept of 'dominion' relates very closely to the idea of a delegated stewardship. In the creation story of Genesis 1, human beings male and female are made in the image, likeness and resemblance of God and are given dominion over created things. They are put in charge with a delegated power from the maker. Since they are in God's image and after his likeness, they will be expected to work selflessly as he does. Thus the dominion is for the good of creation, not for its exploitation. This is a very important stewardship concept, as humanity is faced with the challenge of conservation and the proper use of the earth's resources. Wise stewards have to weigh the contribution each must give to the support and continuation of the human race against the now recognized limits of the resources which have to last a long time. Even oxygen may be in danger of being in short supply. Dominion is for conservation and service, not for exploitation. In the creation story of Genesis 2 man is placed in the garden to cultivate it and to guard it; a responsibility for work and for watchfulness. As the story develops, new characters are introduced, people with special skills who by offering their unique contribution make life tolerable for all. Abel was a shepherd, Cain a farmer, Jabal a nomadic herdsman; then there is the tool maker and the vine dresser and not least Jubal the musician. The whole personality is catered for by the skills imparted through nature to the race.

God's creative gifts and natural skills have still to be used for the benefit of all and not for the self satisfaction of one. Stewards are God's working agents and through them he perpetuates his rule and gives support to his people.

The misuse of limited freedom through jealousy and murder destroys the relationship, leads to seizure of power and usurping of higher authority and the end of responsibility. Then the tyrant can say, 'Am I supposed to care for my brother?'

We can discern in which camp our heart finds rest by considering the challenge of the Brandt Report of 1979 on North–South co-operation for world recovery, which was followed in 1983 by 'Common Crisis'. Here was a modern word to stewards, in a prophetic succession. Many individuals have responded by giving one per cent of their income to world development agencies. The main obstacle to real movement lies in the higher echelons of governments.

Stewards by calling
Still in the Old Testament, the life story of Joseph takes us from the seventeen-year-old boy in charge of sheep and goats as partner with his brothers, right through the period of imprisonment where his attitude won respect from his jailors and fellow prisoners, to the pinnacle of his fame and usefulness. His triumph was to finish up second only to Pharaoh in authority, in charge of all the country. Chosen, be it noted, as 'a man who has God's spirit in him!' Discretion and wisdom would seem to be two necessary marks of the steward.

The call of Moses has a modern ring about it. There must be many who over the years have resisted the demand to think about and respond to the call of God to become a Christian steward. Moses' excuses range over thirty verses in his encounter with his call in Exodus 3 and 4. No one today is called to such a mammoth task, but excuses flow all the same, springing from property rights, personal dislike or disagreement, unwillingness to think through to a conclusion. 'Not me, try someone else' (Exod. 4.13).

The faithful of the Jewish nation honoured God and served

their neighbours through what they earned. They hated bribery and applauded honest acquisition. In fact it was part of a steward's duty to acquire as well as to conserve. Even sacrifice was an act of giving back to God what was his, involving for the giver the forgoing of the right to use and enjoy the surrendered gift. There are repeated exhortations not to forget the lessons of history and the blessings of God. 'Do not forget the Lord your God, do not fail to obey...' (Deut. 8.11).

Hidden away in the Book of Proverbs are words aspiring after the good life, acceptable to God, 'Keep me from lying, and let me be neither rich nor poor. So give me only as much food as I need. If I have more, I might say that I do not need you. But if I am poor, I might steal and bring disgrace upon my God' (Prov. 30.7-9).

No vicarious stewardship

Those who would encourage others in their stewardship must themselves be committed first. David had put a lot of effort in preparing the way for Solomon to take over the building of the temple. He recognized the need for the dedication of every skill to aid the young and inexperienced heir. Having made his own contribution, being himself utterly committed to the task he is able to appeal to others, 'Who else is willing to give a generous offering to the Lord?' (1 Chr. 29). When David wanted the threshing floor which belonged to Araunah, he would not accept it as a gift. Araunah misunderstood the nature of an offering to the Lord; if he were to provide altar, cattle, wood and fire, David would have no part in it. There is no such thing as vicarious stewardship, 'I will not offer to the Lord my God sacrifices that have cost me nothing' (2 Sam. 24.24).

Jesus and money

Turning to the New Testament, we shall not be surprised to learn how often Jesus talked about money in his analysis of the human situation and his understanding of the effect of poverty and the blandishments of wealth on the race. The poor, though always with us, represent a constant challenge that the rest ought to do something about, and he made it clear that largesse was not the only way to give life and dignity to the under-privileged. Hans Küng in his book, *On being a Christian* (Collins, 1977), refers to Jesus' attitude to wealth. 'Jesus . . . did not prescribe for everybody either renunciation of possessions or common ownership. One will sacrifice everything to the poor (Mark 10.21), another will give away half his possessions (Luke 19.8), a third will help with a loan (Luke 6.34, 35). One gives all he has for God's cause (Mark 12.41–44), others are active in serving and caring for the needy (Mark 15.41) and someone else practises apparently foolish prodigality (Mark 14.3–9). Nothing here is legally regulated (page 248).

There is no support in Jesus' teaching for any ideological view of wealth. Human arrangements for its accumulation and distribution are to be controlled simply by moral considerations of justice, righteousness and a widely interpreted love of brother and sister.

He advised his followers to be detached from possessions and to be generous. The rich young man could not take such a parting from the riches which were so much part of himself and went away sorrowful. The difficulty of the rich endeavouring to enter the kingdom was that they were attached to their riches, and the 'eye of the needle' was too narrow for both. In his parables Jesus presents the servant who is a steward as one bearing great responsibility, whose one aim is to be about his master's business even in his absence, ready to welcome him on his return. Trusty and sensible, faithful and wise, such a servant can be put in sole charge and will never neglect a duty towards those he cares for, nor towards the master whose interests he serves.

Variation in ability

The parable of the talents pursues the same train of thought, but recognizes that not every steward has the same capability as the next. The version in Matthew's Gospel is a simpler story than that in Luke. There are three servants and they are each promoted into the position of steward as their master sets out on a journey. He gave to each a share of his property according to the man's ability and would demand a reckoning later according to his ability. This is an important consideration for God's stewards to grasp. They will not be commissioned beyond their ability but will be expected to use all their powers, however limited, in the master's service. In the parable the inevitable day of reckoning comes. The energy and enthusiasm of the first two servants enabled them to double their money. The timidity and misapprehension of the third caused him to use his energy digging a hole to secure his master's money, and there it remained for a long time. The hidden talent cannot be offered back unused. Though God be neither hard nor unreasonable, he cannot be pleased with the waste of opportunity and the dissipation of energy. There is joyful satisfaction for those who demonstrate their wisdom and faithfulness and they are given greater responsibility. Men weep and grind their teeth in darkness over what they might have been, over what they might have done. Here is a quotation from T. W. Manson's *The Sayings of Jesus* (page 245) which sums up what this parable has to say about the relation of the steward to his master. 'Translated into religious terms this means the absolute claim of God upon man. Man himself, all that he has, and all that he can produce, all belong to God. The purpose of man's existence is to serve God, and apart from such service his life is meaningless and worthless. The reward of such service is opportunity for further and larger service; and the worst punishment for failure to serve is just to be deprived of the opportunity to serve at all.'

The responsible attitude

The parable of the good Samaritan is a story used as an answer to a lawyer's question which arose out of a discussion about eternal life. The lawyer embarked on the impossible task of justifying himself by asking, 'Who is my neighbour?' The failure of priest and Levite to take any real account of need condemns those so concerned about their own affairs that they have no time for others. No doubt the Samaritan was a busy man too; he would have had no natural affection for the injured man. It was need that appealed to his sense of responsibility. The need was specific and demanded immediate, definite and once for all action. There was no limit set upon himself by the Samaritan; no allocation of a limited amount of time; no decision to move on after basic first aid. When he stopped he moved out of the demand of his own business and became part of the lonely world of the stricken traveller. He followed up the concentration of his attention by giving freely of his time, of his possessions, oil and wine, his own beast for transport. Arriving with the man at the inn, he parted with his own money and pledged his credit to the innkeeper for any overspending which might prove necessary. The need met a response, 'his heart was filled with pity', and that became a spring for action.

The steward too must be neighbour. An inflexible programme of giving, even if it be a tenth, might inhibit the promptings of pity aroused by a case of deep need. There must always be room for manoeuvre, systematic giving cannot exclude the availability of personal costly care beyond what is planned for.

The place of the tenth

The tithe became an integral part of the religious regulations of the Jewish people. In the early stories of the patriarchs it formed the basis of an agreement between Jacob and God. The references in Deuteronomy and Leviticus define what is liable to the law of tithe; one-tenth of produce belonged to God and was used primarily for the support of the Levites who looked after the temple. The scribes and Pharisees came under the condemnation of Jesus for their insistence on the minutiae of the law of tithe and their disregard of justice, mercy and fidelity. It is possible to conform to generally accepted outward signs of righteousness and yet to be a mean, dishonest and irritable personality. On the other hand the withholding of tithe became a matter of great concern to the holy men who recognized the apostacy of those accommodating themselves to the new thinking which had little place for God. Tithe dodging was a robbery of God and there would be no prosperity until it was corrected. Tithing is a dangerous minefield for the religious.

There have been those who have embraced tithing because of the promise made in the book of Malachi. This is the wide open and inviting door of legalism which confines the spirit and prevents that flexibility which should be the mark of an outward looking and alert Christian steward. There is no legal obligation laid upon a Christian to provide a tenth of his prosperity for God's work. God does not tax his fellow workers, but he does expect wise handling of all that a person possesses. To be safe in the minefield it is necessary to treat the tenth as a starting point for thought and prayer. The result of sensible calculation will prevent putting too great a burden on one and too light a charge on another. There are people for whom a tenth would not be possible in the light of their other necessary commitments. For others the tenth would seem too little to express their gratitude for spiritual wealth and earthly prosperity. For a few the tenth may be about right. There is no answer in the New Testament to the question, 'What shall I give?' The rich young man was asked for the lot. Zaccheus gave half his goods to the poor and promised a fourfold restoration to those he had cheated. Prayer puts the Christian face to face, as it were, with his master and the insight he receives and the decisions he takes must arise from his stewardship of the gospel and his determination to fulfil the will of God. Clearly then, stewardship is not a modern gimmick to extract money from unwilling purses belonging to people who have no faith in God nor any concern for the work of the Church. What is given should be a devoted gift with a touch of sacrifice in it.

Living by Jesus' standards

Two of the chapters in St Paul's second letter to Corinth deal in some detail with the giving aspect of Christian living. Paul is writing mainly to first generation Christians who are in a variety of states of grace, there is little perfection in the company and some matters call for firm treatment. He writes therefore, to an average Christian congregation of people who have accepted the facts about Jesus and the message of good news and desire to live by Jesus' standards. There is no question that Paul writes to ousiders and unbelievers.

He begins, in Chapter 8, with a recital of the circumstances suffered by the churches of Macedonia which could not overcome their joy nor diminish their generosity. There had been no attempt to cajole them into giving, they wanted to be allowed the privilege of sharing in the collection for God's people. Personal involvement sprang out of their relationship with God, to whom they had given themselves as well as making themselves available in hospitality to Paul and his friends. This Macedonian experience is used by Paul to stimulate the Corinthians to prove the reality of their love. Not only have they the example of other Christians but of the Lord himself who laid aside riches and embraced poverty to enrich his followers. Paul tries to find out why there has been delay in Corinth over the collection which seems to have been agreed in principle a year before. Readiness to give must be backed up by effective action. The collection was an act of fellowship within the whole Christian community and giving must be in proportion to what a man has. This collection does not establish a one-way traffic, time may come when givers will become receivers. The Macedonians sanctified their gift by their own self giving and in this they were close to the mind and act of Jesus. A true gift is costly and has part of the giver in it. Such an attitude delivers us from seeing a gift as a duty; it is not the payment of an account. Nor should it provide self-satisfaction. This empties the gift of any meaning for the recipient and appears as a dole, which evokes no gratitude. Sometimes such self-satisfied giving springs from mistaken ideas of privilege or status with an eye to the acclaim of the crowd. The Christian should be under the compulsion of love for God, sharing that divine compassion which 'loved a world and gave a Son'. Generosity cheerfully offered produces gratitude to God and is a reminder of the free gift of Christ.

Chapter 3

Principles to Practice

We have to put gratitude back into giving. Normally we think of gratitude as the response of the recipient to the thoughtfulness and generosity of the giver. If the practice of stewardship is not to lose contact with the principles, then gratitude as a motive for giving must not be lost sight of. It is a matter of deep gratitude to God that the Christian has resources from which he can alleviate the needs and the suffering of others. Without the providential care of God the harvest from earth and sea would cease; man's dependence on his environment is constantly reiterated and as constantly taken for granted. It is not by the strength of his own arms that man has provided wealth for himself.

The proper use of resources
All wealth is a trust from God and when this principle is put into practice it means that God is interested in the way the trust is handled. It is not simply an interest in a part of wealth, but in the handling of all of it. It is possible by special care of the holy token, a designated proportion, to sanctify the rest. No one should fall into the error of supposing that the dedication of a tenth, or more or less, relieves all responsibility for the proper use and disposal of the rest. This would be the manipulation of a regulation for selfish ends. Christians recognize that it is God who gives the power to get wealth. He imparts the abilities and the natural drive of self interest which gets a man moving in self

support. A primitive childish view should give place to an awareness of others who must be considered and not exploited in this activity of self preservation. St Paul encouraged his readers to work with their hands so that they might be able to give to those in need. The example he chose was a thief who must have undergone a radical change to be able to take such advice (Eph. 4.28). Perhaps some people can understand the phenomenon of the giving God more easily as they contemplate past events, rather than their own subjective condition. By looking at some of the apostles, prophets, evangelists, pastors and teachers whom God gave, they see how the people of God have been equipped for a ministry which builds up the Church. This is not a self generated activity but a consequence of the nature of God who gives. Supremely of course, Jesus is seen as the blessing of God the giver to all mankind. God loved the world and gave his Son, the giver of eternal life. Jesus demonstrates this giving nature of God in his own selfless life and his self offering on the Cross with the gifts which flow from that. In the light of eternal truth personal benefit may appear to have little significance, but it is lifted to a higher plane when it is accepted and used as part of God's plan for his world. The denial of self's demands and the willingness to be identified with Jesus leads to a following which affects personality and possessions. Hereafter, whatever such a follower does for another human being is done for Christ. This is the platform upon which true Christian stewardship rests.

Love motivates gratitude

Anyone whose general unthinking attitude in life is to take everything for granted has a long way to go before grasping the principles which lead to practical stewardship. From a very early age responsible parents endeavour to stimulate in their children feelings and expressions of gratitude. The formal 'thank you' has to become a realistic indication of a true feeling. Emotion, in however limited a way, has to be aroused. A gift out of love is met by love-motivated gratitude. But before emotion is touched there has to be some thinking done.

Thought has to be concentrated not simply on the gift, but on the giver and the reason for the gift. For many this thought process is not a long one; faced with a proffered gift, thanks are quickly expressed because 'it is obvious', they would say. Other ground is stonier and it requires a fundamental change of attitude. This can be brought about by a crisis event or by systematic teaching. The person saved from drowning quickly understands why he should feel and endeavour to express his gratitude. Others, and especially two classes of people, need to be taught. Those who are clearly underprivileged compared with the majority of their contemporaries have to be weaned from the bitter attitude which believes it has nothing, and nothing to be grateful for, especially if deformity and lack of skills are added to poverty. For them it is a long haul, perhaps best helped by similarly afflicted people who have discovered a way to fill life with meaning and usefulness. Even the beggar with nothing to give can part with a few grains of rice from his bowl. He can, out of thankfulness for being alive, smile or sing to cheer others on their way. The other group of people who tend to show little gratitude are the pitiable victims of the affluent society. They appear to have access to everything and are little concerned about values and relationships. They believe they owe no man anything and are able to pay for what they want. It is not surprising that for such a one Jesus might advise the surgery which separates the real man from the attachment to his wealth. St James in picturesque manner warns the rich to weep and wail in the face of coming disaster. The wealthy have to learn to distinguish between honest acquisition and ill gotten gains. There is divine interest in the manner of getting as well as the programme of spending.

Joining the chorus of praise

The teaching by sermon, lecture and seminar is intimately involved in the exposition of the truths of the gospel. The study of life cannot be divorced from the doctrine of God who gives it. Gratitude for small things has to move into the realm of understanding and responding to the greater gifts and to the greatest and most mysterious gift of Jesus, the anointed saviour. The chorus of praise in some of the psalms and in the hymnody of the Church help the learner to understand the community's response to the providence of God. Appreciation moves the mind to express its thankfulness and to find means to return the kindness. When gratitude fails to surface, an exchange of gifts becomes a mere commercial transaction, limited to the value of goods involved and carrying no emotional overtones.

The wealthy who have such difficulty over their own feelings of thankfulness, have equal difficulty in understanding why those on whom they like to bestow their favours show no signs of real gratitude. The recipient of a dole can have no friendly feelings. Any gift bereft of love becomes a dole; no one rejoices in the reminder of his poverty from some superior and more fortunate person. Only love makes a gift acceptable and it is the love which generates gratitude. Once a person has come to a proper understanding of his position as the recipient of the goodness of God in his basic equipment and in that graciousness which allows co-operation with God's purposes, then he moves beyond the calculation which tries to equate thanks to the value of the gift, into the realm of generosity in which calculation has no place. We must take account of the conscientious worker who gives of his best that his work may prosper for the glory of God as well as for his own satisfaction over work well done. The gardener does not leave it all to God; he has his own part to play, and until that part is fulfilled the result is a disappointment. God depends upon his people to reflect his image and to pass on to others the benefits which derive from the Father's self giving. Ours are the hands to do his work.

Nothing is permanent on earth
Since we brought nothing into this world and can carry nothing out, it is obvious that we have a limited lease of time and a temporary control of position and possessions. This is another of the important lessons of principle which will affect the way

life is lived. It can put self interest in its proper place and enhance the view of trusteeship, provided the certainty of accountability and judgement is not overlooked. It would be possible, even for a trustee, to mismanage that which was committed to him and lose it all in a welter of waste. Or, being of a shrewder turn of mind, to manipulate it for his own selfish ends. The temporary nature of our charge should remind us of the eternal owner of all that is and control our activity accordingly. There is nothing dull or restrictive about this trusteeship. Timothy is commanded to remind the rich to place their hope in God 'who generously gives us everything for our enjoyment'.

The delegated stewardship which leaves so much to God's agent and gives him a 'free hand' in his limited dominion does include the freedom to enjoy what he possesses or controls. The records of the life of Jesus with his disciples give very broad hints at the enjoyment of their lives and activities, as characteristic of their fellowship. Humour and laughter hover at the edges of what is written and contradict so much of the oil and water colour impressions of Christ among men. Life is precious, health is a blessing, work a fulfilment, companionship a joy, adventure a thrill. Time did not seem to dominate their lives. The periods of morning, afternoon and evening were not divided up and measured in split seconds. They were under no compulsion to save time or to use time. It is conceivable that the expression 'to waste time' would have been meaningless to them. The puritan error which can only see things in terms of their usefulness and frowns upon what is simply pleasurable is not discernible in the lifestyle of Jesus and his friends. It was not necessary to add luxury to the sustaining strength of the five loaves, but the two fish made the meal more palatable and thus more enjoyable.

There is a temptation in some stewardship thinking to become too obsessed by responsibility to use resources rather than to share the enjoyment of them. Balance is needed and a right attitude quickly corrects any tendency to become selfish in enjoyment which might lead to an ungodly squandering of resources. There is much talk about a Christian lifestyle nowadays. It is good for Christians to have a conscience about their responsibilities for neighbour, but to embrace asceticism for its own sake, and as a consequence to wear a dull and sullen face, will do nothing to commend the following of Christ. We do well to remember the father's words to his elder son in the parable 'Son, you are always with me, and all that I have is yours' (Luke 15.31).

Avarice, gluttony and envy are still among the deadly sins and, when embraced, have a devastating and disintegrating effect upon the human spirit. They have no place in the life style of the Christian who, delivered from them by the victory of Christ, is enriched by all the good gifts, material, aesthetic and spiritual, so freely bestowed by a smiling providence.

Faith in God's providence

This is a very important principle, that God does supply every need. This must be related to the search for God's kingdom, as Jesus has said. We should not worry ourselves sick about the morrow. Nevertheless it is a principle hard to grasp and can only become a practical part of everyday living by a continuing act of faith. Faith is not as the schoolboy described it, a faculty which adults have for believing the impossible. Basically it is a confident trust in the being and character of God as revealed in Jesus. It has in it, as well, the ingredient of obedience. Out of this confidence in God, many steps of faith may be taken in obedience to the promptings of the Spirit, and each one strengthens the certainty of God's care and the resolve to do things God's way. Sometimes a stewardship campaign is embarked upon because of complete unbelief in this matter. 'God will not supply', they think, 'and so we must act ourselves.' Fund-raising proceeds and some sort of result ensues, which neither honours God nor satisfies the need which prompts the campaign.

Stewardship is not practised simply within the context of a campaign mounted by a church, or even by a community for a project for the improvement of the life of its members. It is practical in its relationship to the environment on planet earth and, very soon, in man's exploitation of his galaxy, as well as in its concern for the inhabitants of this global village. This does not mean that the Christian steward must subscribe to, and become personally involved with every society which has a limited concern for some aspect of environmental con-servation. But he ought to know what is going on and be alert to speak out when necessary, and to give financial and personal aid where that is appropriate. The 'common crisis' in the relationship between the wealthy and the poor has already been referred to. This is a very urgent matter if we are to leave the world in good order for the enjoyment of our successors. Not many can be involved in top level discussions or in the making of a manifesto, but all can be aware, through a right attitude engendered by the acceptance of the basic principles of stewardship.

Money and its uses

In the twentieth century we are all dominated by a money economy, and although barter may be practised in some places and through some transactions, the getting, exchanging, and spending of money takes up a great deal of energy and planning. We cannot get away from money. It is not an evil in itself. Its use has developed over the centuries and it has become representative of the real goods and services which make up so much of life's transactions. It can be used for good or evil purposes, but those purposes are conceived in the minds of human beings. Basic attitudes control these thoughts and plans, for it is from the heart of man 'that come the evil ideas which lead him to do immoral things' (Mark 7.21). As Timothy is told 'the love of money is a source of all kinds of evil'. It is a love which entices all alike, and with sadness it is recalled that 'some have been so eager to have it that they have wandered away from the faith and have broken their hearts with many sorrows' (1 Tim. 6.10).

Money needs to be controlled, and a good way for individuals and corporations is to budget for a proper record of income and control of expenditure. Everything can then be done decently and in order. A comparison with accounts a year later can show how closely intention was matched by achievement. Some other parts of the Anglican Communion can teach us about budgeting which allocates a large percentage of income for God's work in pioneer places. Those who choose to operate the tithe on diocesan or parish accounts, not only pass resolutions to do so, but actually fulfil that intention. The same cannot be said about similar resolutions from some diocesan synods. Others go beyond the tenth and work towards a standard which allocates a dollar to be given away for every dollar retained at home. One can imagine the cries of pain such a proposal would evoke in a sterling area!

Sacrificial giving

Yet from earliest times sacrifice has been a large part of worship, even though it was accounted worthless apart from moral goodness. Practice must reflect the underlying principles which relate to the 'agency role' of human beings. What is lent has to be administered. This ministry is not remote and cold, it must be supported by the warmth of human concern prompted by love and in the light of conscience. A conscience can become sensitive in a prayerful life, and love can open eyes to need more readily than the need itself. There is no sacrifice in the dedication of a portion which allows the rest to be dissipated into thoughtless waste. The portion should consecrate the whole and not be treated as a tax to relieve of all subsequent responsibility.

Self interest, any sort of vested interest, may prove a dangerous threat to any kind of steward, whether he profess the name of Christian or not. The ordinary man with no specific religious convictions will find it hard to care for himself, his folk or his world, if the motives of worldly enrichment threaten his higher aspirations. It is worse when the Christian forgets his master and manipulates his wealth and position for his own aggrandizement. He will never see the naked, hungry, thirsty or imprisoned. He is among those condemned to hear, 'Depart from me, I never knew you'.

When St Paul was arranging for the collection which was to relieve the necessity of the poor Christians in Jerusalem he gave guidelines which have been followed by those who were determined to discharge their Christian giving in a worthy manner.

1. First of all, giving must not be haphazard; it demands thought.
2. So it must be in proportion to what he has earned in the matter of wages; and, no doubt, in the matter of savings to what he has put by.
3. The proportion has not to be niggardly but generous and the way to guarantee this is to approach giving as the Macedonians did, 'First they gave themselves to the Lord and then... they gave themselves to us as well'.
4. Commitment produces generosity (2 Cor. 8.5). St Paul has much to teach in this Epistle to the Corinthians of the open handed generosity of God. Generous giving meets people's need and brings glory to God because it proves loyalty to the gospel of Christ.
5. A further characteristic is cheerfulness, which overcomes negative feelings of regret at having to give or the acceptance of a supposed duty to give. 'God loves the one who gives gladly' (2 Cor. 9.7).
6. Because giving should be the result of decision it will be full of meaning for the giver and will demonstrate his purpose to glorify God. There is therefore to be purpose in giving.
7. Towards the recipient there must be proof of love (2 Cor. 8.24). God's interest does not cease when income is allocated to swell capital. It does not matter how the decision about proportion is followed up. The money may be given immediately or saved up for some special occasion, such as St Paul envisages when

it is to be given to those who will carry it to Jerusalem. For the Christian when he gives, the critical moment is that of decision about the proportion. The method of passing it on whether by envelope, covenant, cash or cheque is a matter of administration and much less important (1 Cor. 16.2).

Misuse of money

Money can be used, of course, to escape responsibility and to buy immunity from demands of charity. There is a complete lack of principle in that kind of practice. Generosity certainly does not enter into it, neither does proportionate giving related to prosperity; it is empty of meaning or purpose, has nothing to do with love and cannot be honouring to God. As faith is demonstrated by works, love is confirmed by gift; but, as faith without works is dead, so is a gift without love. Archbishop Ramsey writing to his diocese at the close of his time in Canterbury said, 'We face dangerous times amidst spiritual apathy around us. One need is a revival of stewardship and I believe it will be happening. The greatest need is a deeper sacrifical and joyful commitment to the Lord whom we serve.'

The characteristic of a God of love is that he gives. We who are made in his image will find no satisfaction in our possessions or our relationships unless we acknowledge our own need to follow our God in his giving. We do this, as the Archbishop said, in a deeply sacrificial and joyful commitment to our Lord.

Chapter 4

Motivation

The Lambeth bishops reminded the Church that God had already given his people all the human and financial resources necessary to carry out his mission in the world. By saying that, they pointed to the overriding motive for the activity of a committed Christian, to support, encourage and further God's mission in the world. Many Christians have long been convinced of this and have by personal dedication of service and money provided manpower and finance for that mission. The stewardship project is a means of introducing many others to the challenge of the gospel. For over twenty years the subject of Christian stewardship has been endeavouring to edge its way on to the Church's agenda. It received attention at Lambeth in 1958, 1968 and 1978. Over those years a great deal of thought had gone into the meaning and implication of this subject. Much work had been done on its theological background and on its practical application in church life. In that time stewardship should have become part of the normal processes of thought and activity of all Christian people. The reality is that the impact of the idea has been intermittent, sporadic and not at all universal. Section 3 of Lambeth 1978 delivered the following very important statement: 'God himself is the almighty resource of the Church. Our feeble prayers are necessary but are only made effectual by being mingled with those of him who ever liveth to make intercession for us. We believe that prayer relying upon the Holy Spirit must be the spiritual basis of any plan of action in the Church. We claim that God has already given his people all the human and financial resources necessary to carry out his mission in the world. The problem persists that so many skills remain uncommitted and so much money remains firmly in the pockets of Church members. A greater degree of realism about what sacrificial giving means, and a wider sharing of knowledge, skills and resources is called for. People should give according to the measure of their love for God and their understanding of the gospel. We need to study motivation and encourage Christians to give and serve for the right reasons.'

A wider vision

In the face of such a statement of faith as that it is difficult to imagine why a good deal of stewardship teaching in the Church of England has not passed beyond the stage of fund-raising, an appeal to people to meet the needs of the institutional Church. If God is our resource and if he has already given his people all the human and financial resources he needs to carry out his mission, then it is time that deeper consideration should be given to what his mission is and how best we may use the manpower resources which are there to be offered to him. The principles of Christian stewardship are concerned much more with the motive for giving than with the needs which have to be met by thanksgiving. If the ultimate aim is the glory of God and the extension of his mission in the world, then the Church's teaching must lift the minds of its people beyond the economics of parish finance into the realm of devotion and sacrifice which involves not only the giving of resources for the work of God but the devotion of the whole personality into the service of God in the world. A wider vision is required that will embrace a proper understanding of the conservation of the world's resources. One of the ways in which that conservation can become a personal matter is for the individual to practise the proper conservation of his own resources of money, time and energy. Giving by Christians was a subject which occupied the minds of the leaders of the Church before the Gospels were written. St Paul has a great deal to say about the Christian's attitude to his money. When the Gospels are examined it is quite clear that Jesus looked upon wealth as a powerful factor and revealed a great deal about the character of people who had to handle it. The care of the underprivileged has always been a Christian concern and the benevolences of past generations still have their effect on the society of today. Of course, there were occasions when the successors of the Pharisees, who stood on the street corners playing trumpets about their charity, built religious institutions and churches more to the glory of man than the glory of God. A Christian gospel has never envisaged that the privilege of giving should be confined to those who had a surplus. In the earliest days the Thessalonians gave beyond their means to the collection that was going to help succour the needs of others in a worse state than themselves, and the generosity of the widow has become a lasting sign for those who would understand what sacrificial giving is all about.

Avoid unworthy motives

The road to commitment to Christ is for some people a very long one which may begin by the finding of some ill-defined track leading on to a firmer path until the full realization of what walking the narrow way may mean. What the patrons of a stewardship effort must avoid is the appeal to unworthy motives. To appeal to self interest or human pride does nothing for the cause and puts God in a poor light. Our Victorian forbears were great believers in the acknowledgement of gifts from lists of donors (with amounts) in the local paper. A target could be reached by a community effort 'to keep up with the Joneses!' Emulation or a desire to retain one's place in society has little to do with the glory of God. In fund-raising the most frequent basis of appeal is the need to be met by the donations of well wishers. The hospice movement which grows so rapidly throughout the nation is dependent on voluntary contributions for establishment and maintenance and is a proper object for generous support. But the need of the institutional Church is less than a worthy motive for giving by a Christian steward. He is not simply concerned with raising funds for particular objects. His task is to distribute the money he has allocated after thought and prayer for the work of God and for general benevolence. He will respond to emerging need either out of his 'giving away budget' or, on occasion, beyond it. Fund-raising is perfectly respectable but must not be confused with the wider concept of stewardship, to the detriment of both. Funds may be raised by a wide variety of activity, stewardship challenges to the direct giving of money and the employment of personal skills.

There are people who devote themselves to the well-being of others. Heroic stories are told of doctors and nurses, of police and welfare workers, of people in all walks of life who abandon all claim to their own comfort and safety for others' sakes. Mother Teresa of Calcutta has been in the news, recognized and honoured. She would claim that she was only doing something quite natural. Onlookers may say with great admiration that they are no Mother Teresa, yet they would be wrong to exclude themselves from the possibility of care for others. There is in every human being a deep need to give. It may become obscured in this materialistic and selfish world, but it is there to be awakened. When love comes to life its highest aspiration is to give to the beloved. It dies when the lust to take usurps love's place in the heart. The giver needs to give; the servant needs to serve. This cannot be said of the miser or the slave, the freedom of personal choice will have been surrendered or lost.

Much of the appeal from the Church, local and national, seems to spring from a form of panic which sees the disaster of bankruptcy looming. The calculated sum needed for rescue is published and divided among the membership. So much per head would put the books right. This may clear a deficit, but it does not help the expanding work of the kingdom of God. The theology of Christian stewardship must be taught lest the activist element in the Church tries to use stewardship as a means of discharging an obligation which in fact can never be discharged.

No threat to the gospel

Serious challenge has been offered to the stewardship idea by people whose dedication to the gospel could never be doubted. To these Bible students there is the danger that stewardship as practised could be a threat to the gospel, elbowing its way to the centre of the stage and taking the limelight from the great acts of God in Christ. Salvation for sale at 50 pence a week or a three year agreement to pay are expressions of appalling heresy. If that error is masquerading as Christian stewardship it must be driven out. Most people will not have seen a stewardship campaign in that light, but finely tuned theological minds are bound to be alert to any perversion. There have been schemes where it was blatantly plain that 'it is your money we are after and no questions asked (or answered)'. The benefactor of the institution who appears in church three times a year and gives the rector a substantial cheque in April may be an admirable character but his view of his place in the church is not couched in Bible terms and does not reflect the standards of Jesus. No stewardship parish could bear to leave him stranded in his ignorance, but would want to bring him along from where he is to a proper understanding of his potential as a son and steward of God. Stewardship properly understood keeps the evangelistic note sounding in the congregation. The gospel itself is the standard by which stewardship has to be tested. When a campaign is mounted with the object of providing funds for the comfort or enjoyment of the congregation, it is simply a means of self help—and may even list its needs and appeal to its constituency to see that charity should begin at home. Modern heating or a multi-manual organ may be matters that have to be deferred in the light of the expanding demands of the kingdom of God. The abolition of targets will avoid all possibility of misunderstanding. The simple challenge to all must be that they should match their giving to their devotion. When the giving is casual the problem lies with the devotion.

Moved by gratitude

Perhaps the most generally understood reason for accepting the stance of a steward in God's affairs is that of thankfulness. A person does not need to be a qualified theologian to assess the many reasons he has in life to be thankful. For those who consider that there is nothing special for which they have to be thankful an hour of honest minutes looking at themselves and listing their blessings should have a profound effect. How much better off he may be than his out-of-work neighbour. How much better off the healthy neighbour than the bedridden woman up the street. So it could go on, and when material blessings have been listed there are the spiritualities as they are expressed in human love and friendship, and above all in the condescension of almighty God in his giving of Christ and his supply of the Holy Spirit. Cost and price may apply to things; these must be left behind and only the spiritual will remain. 'What is seen is temporal what is unseen is eternal' (2 Cor. 4.18).

A Christian stewardship project should be planned in such a way that those participating should be stimulated to think of gratitude. This will banish casualness and lack of concentration in the necessary preparation. Those who are to visit others must themselves have thought through their thanksgiving to God for 'creation, preservation and all the blessings of this life; but above all, for thine inestimable love in the redemption of the world by our Lord Jesus Christ' (BCP General Thanksgiving). They should also have experienced the motivation which such thinking gives and have followed motivation through to response in terms of money and call to special service.

Trouble with money
Some people are inhibited when dealing with the money aspect of Christian stewardship. Some hidden prejudice holds them back from seeing money in its true neutral light, as an instrument which may be used for good or evil by those who possess it. Money has a different look according to the way it is travelling. That which comes our way is welcome, attractive and full of promise of what it could do. When we are parted from it, see it pass beyond our grasp and use, thoughts become resentful. Nobody really loves the faceless inspector of taxes—

imagination makes of him a sour spectacle taking life blood and leaving the victim weak and frustrated. Of course it is never as bad as that, but humans do enjoy their fantasies. It is sad when those who mount a Christian stewardship campaign are thought of as invaders of privacy, as extractors of that substance that makes life worth living. Instead, if their labour is dedicated to the honour of God and if they have faced the challenge themselves, they come with ideas which release a person from the bonds of anxiety reaching around him from the false aura of money. Money matters, not on account of what it is, but because of what it can do. The resistance to thinking about money must be overcome, not only in those who feel themselves threatened, but also in those who find it difficult to talk about it. Some are prepared to use much talk about time and talents to wrap up consideration of money, thus indicating that it is an unspiritual commodity.

Time and skill

The use of talent and ability is a separate issue. There are some aspects of Christian stewardship which cannot be dealt with by money, they demand personal involvement and physical or mental effort. Nor can time be treated as a commodity to be divided up among conflicting demands. The proper use of time keeps it holy. Giving an hour to God once a week and forgetting him for the rest is no proper stewardship. Most of a breadwinner's time is spent winning bread. The whole of that time can be an offering of daily work to God. Reflecting the standards of Jesus in the processes of daily business can be a powerful witness to colleagues and contemporaries who learn to accept and trust God's man in business. They do not welcome pious phraseology or 'holier than thou' attitudes, but they do recognize and applaud a man whose word is to be trusted, who speaks truth and builds relationships on a firm foundation of respect and care. A person spending forty odd hours a week working 'as to the Lord', has no need to respond to pressure to commit his spare time to some non-productive church work. There will be those qualified to do so, who will volunteer to use some time and a particular talent meeting some worthwhile need. Let money stand alone, the power of Christ has redeemed it for the kingdom and dealt with materialistic thinking surrounding it. In a modern economy its presence, its temptations, and its power for good or ill must be faced, and Christ's victory claimed by every Christian steward who cannot avoid handling it. When a man gets the right attitude to money, he is making rapid progress to a well co-ordinated personality.

Conviction about principles

The responsibility which rests upon those planning a Christian stewardship campaign is a heavy one. They must themselves be convinced about the spiritual realities upon which stewardship practice should be built. They must also be clear about what the motives are to be for those to be asked to become part of the scheme. Self interest, self satisfaction, holding back all but an unworthy token, even the pressing needs of the church must give place to an appeal to the gratitude of the giver. Thankfulness is a great stimulant and leads to generosity which can be startling. Years ago a poor Bible woman gave her week's tithe and her life's savings to help forward a mission plan. Despite her vicar's remonstration that so much was too much, she insisted. Such giving was noticed outside the temple treasury when the poor widow put in all her living. In the relatively modern case the noticing was followed by an unexpected legacy which more than replaced the gift. God is no man's debtor.

Those whose motives are always self regarding need a radical change of heart which cannot be brought about by argument. No argument could have led St Paul out of darkness into light. It needed a spiritual encounter which affected him deep in his spirit. No peripheral change would have done. The change of mind and direction had to be complete. St Paul saw the Lord and heard the gospel. In a similar fashion there must be a change of attitude in those unmoved by the bounty of the creator, or the loving generosity of a redeemer. It is very unlikely that a stewardship campaign would bring about such a radical change of heart, but a combination of good teaching and the witness of those who respond generously to the love of God may produce a spark of interest, which with wisdom and care might become a flame to burn up selfishness. The Holy Spirit meets the prayers of God's people and does his own strange work.

The starting point of involving parishioners in a stewardship project is their own estimation of themselves. If a start is made there, complaints are out of place. If a person claims to belong, then membership should be accepted as a fact; no one should be allowed to judge the value of such self assessment (and least of all the incumbent). If he says he believes in God and Christ; if he is seen, however infrequently, in church; if he wants to be treated as all the others are, then no approach to him could be called an intrusion. It will have been made because of his willingness to be identified as a churchman. We must expect growth in grace even from small beginnings.

Chapter 5

Barriers to Understanding

It sometimes occurs that a stewardship project is mounted in such a way that the object of the exercise is obscured because of hazy vision and administrative complication. The promoters believe that within a church context more than money should be involved. They are not quite sure what these other areas are, nor what is their relationship to the obtrusive realities of parish finance. It springs sometimes from a sharp distinction between what the vicar does and what the lay folk are able to do. Perhaps the vicar does it all and is poor at delegating to his people; alternatively, the vicar may be overwhelmed by ecclesiastical laymen who leave him no freedom to pursue his calling, demanding such cossetting that he has no time for evangelism or pastoral care.

In the early days it was the complaint of those who could see great potential in properly conducted stewardship campaigns that campaigns were undertaken for all the wrong reasons, the main one being an acute shortage of money. A campaign should issue from a congregation well taught in gospel truths and desirous of expressing their devotion and gratitude to almighty God. Satisfaction should attend a project consisting of helpful teaching and an opportunity for quiet self examination of attitudes to wealth and responsibility. A project should help people to be aware of the resources of manpower and money within the worshipping congregation and to realize, because of others' experience, that dedicated resources are enough to meet obvious needs and newly disclosed opportunities of service. The campaign should discover what is available, not what is wanted. Targets of need are not required; the target of giving may well be the tithe so long as it is seen, not as a tax, but as a starting point for thought and prayer.

Opening the closed mind

No one is going to be gripped by an idea if they refuse to contemplate it. One of the barriers to understanding quite common among our people is the closed mind. Content for many years to adopt a method of 'church support' by 'pay as you go', grown men, successful in business, react as dogs to a bell when called to 'let your light so shine before men that they may see your good works'. In some cases inflation has changed the coin into a note, but low denomination notes and coins are still considered sufficient for the demonstration of good works. The question of glorifying God does not seem to enter into the picture. The closed mind cannot grasp the stewardship challenge, but in a variety of ways will endeavour to justify itself. Some do so by a comparison with others, whose circumstances they can only guess at. Others believe they are too heavily committed, but will not examine the areas of commitment to see how investment in them would win the approval of God. 'I cannot afford it' springs out of a conviction that the prison bars of poverty have them firmly locked in.

There is a person who likes to give the impression that he is interested and would like to do more and, when he gets the time or has a surplus in his cash flow, he will act. Time is apt to demand the continuing of the accepted round into which it is well nigh impossible to insert more activity. Impossible, of course, until some less important matter gives place to beneficial action. Who has ever heard of anyone with a surplus from which he will distribute gifts for God and needy neighbour? The demands of the electronic revolution present themselves before a surplus appears. Even the plastic money offers to take the wait out of want! Some people are sure that they are spontaneous givers; they like to feel moved by a present need whether it be to aid animals or children. 'I am large hearted. I respond to an appeal to my emotions.' There are still some of this type left, although the media by presenting death, mutilation and disaster tend to deaden sensitivity.

Giving away can be viewed as such a private thing that in church bags are preferred to plates, and a treasury at the door an even better thing. 'What a man gives', they say, 'is between himself and his God.' Often there is very little between a man and his God, and it is to correct this state of affairs that stewardship presents its challenge at every level and not only to that which is material.

St Thomas Aquinas, a thirteenth century theologian, had a view of property which casts a bright beam upon some twentieth century views of charity. He insisted that human laws must not prevent provision being made for the poor. Nor was there any merit in giving away goods surplus to need. Much charitable giving which tends to leave a happy glow in the giver, is simply the clearing out of wardrobes, cupboards and lofts to make room for new, modern and fashionable substitutes. There is no sacrifice in surplus-to-need giving and, if merit there is, it is only that it prevents waste. (Although cold and starving Africans find western cast-offs difficult to manage.) Mary Magdalene could have used the box of ointment for herself but she sacrificed it all in her devotion to Jesus. The widow in the treasury put in all her living. When people are young it seems to be an acceptable part of their growing up that they are always after the next thing. There is an ambition to possess as well as to get on. Someone has called this the adoration of the unpossessed. The young man's bicycle has to be exchanged for one with an engine; then comes the turn of the three-wheeler, then the Mini. By this time the young man should have grown up, but he does not grow out of the modern idolatry. He strives for bigger, better, newer in cars, and size in houses, more select in environment and (most miserably) young and prettier in wives. Much of this may be beyond his resources to support and he finds himself bearing the burdensome weight of poverty which keeps pace with every salary increase that comes his way.

Release through commitment
The secret history of the human stories coming out of stewardship teaching and projects could tell of many prosperous and worldly people being so gripped by the reality of God's being and love that they have made a response to the invitation of Jesus to receive release, reconciliation and new life. The mockery of the unpossessed loses its fascination, and one here, one there is free to enjoy the life of a child of God.

Christians who are keen to obey the mission instructions of Jesus sometimes feel disappointment that the evangelistic note is not sounded in stewardship campaigns. Perhaps it is that they want the note to sound louder, for it is certainly there. One diocesan missioner noticed that there could be a greater spiritual response from a well mounted stewardship project than a ten day evangelistic mission. It must represent the best in administration and teaching and it must be addressed to people who see themselves as those within the sound of the gospel. No stewardship campaign which goes for the real outsider can possibly be termed evangelistic. The preparation for evangelism is a long process demanding patience and sensitivity. Contact cannot be casual between people belonging to the same community. Points of contact and degrees of understanding vary from place to place and people to people. The gospel has to be demonstrated; often the least important aspect is the verbalizing.

It is quite a different matter to expect some impact upon nominal members of a congregation from stewardship teaching. The aim of evangelism is to obtain a verdict and a commitment from those who are approached with the gospel. The clear aim must be supported by prayer, adequate preparation and hard work. If this aim to make better Christians is incorporated in the planning, the campaign will remain within the continuing mission of the church. A church congregation does not become evangelistically minded by an occasional sortie into some kind of mission. The mission whether based in stewardship or gospel preaching has to be an expression of the never ceasing application of life and witness to the commission of Jesus to his followers. The church through its members has to 'go' before the message will register as an invitation to 'come'. The nominal must become committed to a real relationship with God through Christ which will issue in conscious membership of his body as a spirit guided person. From such commitment effective witness can emerge. The steward's care of himself and his possessions is a spiritual consequence of such commitment. Many people are inarticulate and their understanding slow to grow. Whatever their response may be it should be welcomed, in the hope that growth may turn service and gift into a holy token representing the whole of the life and personality of the steward. When God is at work the finest thread of response will be used to draw men to himself. The church by its prayer and faith co-operates with God in this loving ministry. The church lines itself up with God's concern for people and will resist any fund-raising effort which is concerned only with numbers, with pounds and pence and a profit on the exercise. Money is either upholstery to make members comfortable or it is power to make the church effective. Yet money is never enough as a target, it must represent the interest and care of people. Information must be provided to feed that interest, telling what is happening at home and abroad as a result of prayerful giving. This can help deliver from the parochial mind which cannot look beyond the closest boundaries.

Stewardship in mission

These islands have a complicated history and we are now emerging from the trauma of losing, or giving up, an empire. In the luxurious days when raw materials came to these shores from all the lands under the sun not many questions were asked about conditions in those lands, except by Christians who saw opportunities for gospel preaching and church expansion if they were to follow the flag. Looking back, their successors are embarrassed by the attitudes they adopted and the mistakes they made. Paternalism in the secular power was emulated by the representatives of the Lord. The hungry offered faith in exchange for rice. Ancient religions were written off as expressions of paganism, and arrogance obscured the loving face of Jesus. The reaction to all this has erected barriers against missionary support. Societies struggle to maintain their work and find themselves short of manpower. The emphasis has changed, of course, and more is heard of humility and partnership. The excitement of mission in the world for Christ has died or become very subdued in the hearts of the men and women in the pew. The Partners in Mission project in many dioceses has had the effect of putting a new face on mission endeavour, and has linked the need of ongoing evangelism at home with the support for expansion in the younger Churches. Information reaches us too, of the glowing fire of Christian spirituality in Russia where, despite all the oppression, opposition and difficulties, thousands attend the Liturgy of the Orthodox, and Baptist ranks are constantly swelling. Revival of interest will come as information is absorbed, and prayer will follow, stimulating minds to explore what more can be done.

When stewardship teaching and the mounting of a campaign is undertaken for the greater glory of God, the pastoral and evangelistic intent becomes apparent. It is this aspect rather than any claim on a person to review his financial position that presents a barrier to wholehearted participation. The English character at times is oppressed by a sense of unworthiness when confronted with the invitations of God, and rather than venture forth, he holds back. It is important that this side of a steward's responsibility should not be neglected. St Paul wanted himself and his fellow Christians to be thought of as stewards of God's secret truths. The good news revealed by Jesus is precious and must be shared. In the declaration of what a man knows of God's way the steward is to be faithful in the performance of his duty in his master's name. The call to be a witness can be more disturbing than a call which seems to be limited to a material response. The reiteration of the basic truths of the gospel make the challenge clearer, and in every field God asks only something of what a man has, not of what he has not. The gifts of the Spirit and the functions within the body of Christ are offered for his faithful use, and in accepting them he finds his true place. Such a possibility of service seems to some so far beyond them that they would rather not think about it. It is so much easier to sign a cheque, or take out a covenant than to become personally involved in church fellowship and community care. The challenge to take the sacramental life seriously and to include Bible reading and prayer in a daily discipline is for some too much to ask, and they close their minds to it.

The lay person's spirituality
Some investigation into the Bible reading habits of church people has produced startling results, showing what a low priority this has with so many. The excuse that the Bible is too difficult to understand will not hold water in the light of the excellent help produced by such aids as the Scripture Union and the Bible Reading Fellowship. A proper understanding of what the gospel is will engage heart and head. Thus it is essential that total dependence on short Sunday sermons shall not become the main plan for teaching. The Bible has to be read by individuals, studied in groups and always approached in a prayerful atmosphere. The religious exercises can degenerate into a dull routine, but an awakened life can see them, and use them, as a means of worship and spiritual growth. Attitudes have to be changed equally as facts have to be absorbed.

There are those who go through life without having time to give serious thought to the meaning of their existence and destiny. A stewardship campaign ought to provide the material for such thought. To limit the effort to a cash collection for a needy institution misses the golden opportunity. Many have found a change of heart as they have probed deeply into the reasons which lie behind the presentation of the stewardship idea. The number of adult confirmation candidates who have come forward as a result of pastoral interest generated by a stewardship project is an indication of this.

Teaching young people

When you have not grown up with an idea it comes as a shock or a surprise when confronted with it in later life. Children should not be kept in ignorance of the relationship of stewardship to Christian living. Nowadays many children have a very poor start in their education relating to the Christian faith. State education tries to be fair to all and as a consequence there is in some schools an endeavour to cover the main tenets of the major religions, and Christianity is treated as one option among many. Even in church schools the facts about the life, death and resurrection of Jesus are sometimes treated in a purely historical sense and there is little application to the demands of everyday life. This is not so in every school, of course, and where the Christian faith is taught and demonstrated by Christian teachers there is a sound foundation laid for life. But the stewardship idea took a long time to be revived in mature Christian circles and it seems to be taking even longer to be shared with our children. The endeavour in stewardship campaigns to obtain the involvement of all the family should include the children. The children in one family were consulted about having a share in the weekly offering and agreed to a proportion of pocket money to be 'given to God'. A wise father doubled the pocket money allocation to make the arrangement realistic and thereafter refused all requests for money for the collection. A parish has reported great encouragement from the group of teenage visitors who took responsibility for friends of their own age. As adults cannot leave it to the squire, so the young may not leave it all to their elders.

The young must learn that stewardship is part of the normal lifestyle of a serious Christian. This will prevent future surprise and a natural reaction to avoid some new demand.

Perhaps the greatest barrier to a happy conclusion to a campaign is the isolation of money from its context. It is important, but its importance does not lie in itself. It represents the character of the people who handle it. Its power lies in what it can do. Money becomes mammon when it is cut adrift from its source and is unrelated to its use. An instrument must never become an idol.

Chapter 6

Individual and Corporate Responsibility

In the majority of cases the word of the Lord in the Old Testament was addressed to national groups, to Israel or Judah or surrounding nations. In the New Testament the word from Jesus or his apostles is for large and small crowds, groups of listeners or newly formed churches. The opportunity which such a declaration provides is related more closely to intensity than duration. Never to the alert God-fearing mind does it occur that 'there is plenty of time'. The future did not stretch into infinity, there was the expectation of an end, a reckoning, a parousia. The word of the Lord presents the listener with an immediate crisis. A response is required which cannot be put off. One of the ways in which God has been speaking to his Church over the last thirty years has been through the stewardship movement. This has been closely followed by, and may well be closely connected with, the renewal movement with its startling phenomena in all branches of the Church.

God's word for today

God has been speaking to his Church. He calls us all to come out of our poverty, to slough off our inability to do what we should be doing for him. He speaks that we may recognize that our physical poverty is merely an expression of our spiritual poverty. If we will listen, turn around and go back to him, then his power will release us to get on with our work for him. We have listened to the word of stewardship because the shoe pinches. We are inhibited in what ought to be ordinary and natural expressions of our Christian care for others. The devoted service of the Church is hindered by lack of resources. It is an important precept that 'stewardship should teach people how to express their devotion', but care must be taken not to debase it by translating devotion into cash in order to make life easier. This is to mistake 'pressure' for 'devotion' and to keep us in the shallowest waters of thought about stewardship.

Despite the growth of the Christian Church in parts of the so called third world, the light of Christian truth is being quenched in many places. The world-wide society of the people of God does not grow in relation to the increasing world population. Does it matter? What difference does being a Christian make? If the difference is not apparent it is because of spiritual apathy, of poverty in the riches of Christ. The promises are ignored and the power is not tapped. Where is the warmth and welcome of Church fellowship? Another sign of our poverty is the continuing depressed numbers of offers for ordination. The gaps are beginning to show and God wants them filled by the right kind of tough people who will not resist a call to a tough assignment. There is a danger here that successful money raising may take sacrifice out of vocation and open the door so wide that, despite the Advisory Council, some potentially unhappy people may slip through. In matters of vocation the Church is up against the blandishments of a worldliness which says, 'Money matters. Returns matter. Security is priceless.' Christian parents, as a consequence, view the call to the ministry as a disaster for son or daughter.

The impact of the Church
The word of the Lord through stewardship would have something to say about the impact of the Church on community life. Leading articles in newspapers may not always

reflect the thinking of ordinary people, but recently they have been scathing about the place of the Church and its feeble thrust. Concerned too much about internal matters, the Church talks to itself, ignoring God and the world. Others, of course, would applaud the withdrawal of church spokesmen from the public arena, and tell them to get back to the business of getting people to heaven. It is impossible to win, but listening to criticism can lead to constructive action. We live in a world that is dying for God, as a man would die for lack of water. To such a world Jesus says, for his Church to proclaim, 'I am the resurrection and the life'. The destroyers of the twentieth century are not in the same category as the Black Death. They are the new widely held beliefs about abortion on demand; divorce after a year's trial; pornography available by personal choice, genetic engineering without moral sanctions or ethical guidelines; the ominous rise of unemployment, and the impact on it of long hours and much overtime; the breakdown of relationship between management and workforce; and, in many parts of the world, government by the edict of a caucus or a dictator. The list is not comprehensive, but it indicates areas where God would have his Church champion the rights of the people.

The word of stewardship may say that a poor Church is better able to do so than a rich one. There is a poverty which is holy and not inhibiting. It has enough to manage on and is lavish in its distribution of the rest. Riches in a spiritual organization are an affront to the common man. In the centuries when the Church was rich and comfortable it became deaf to the voice of God and seldom spoke itself in protest. The road to martyrdom was chosen by the inspired few who could see wickedness for what it was. The warning of dangerous ground must therefore be sounded, lest the motivation for a Christian stewardship project should be a selfish one. It is all right to get the money right so as to clear the decks for action as a church in the world for the world. It would be quite wrong just to go for cushioned tip-up seats in place of the old pews!

Stewardship must not be limited by narrow horizons and

tight boundaries. The world is the Christian's concern. It was the world which God loved. It was for humanity that Christ died. Those who recognize themselves as stewards for God, are in the great succession of the prophets and fellow workers. By life and lip they proclaim Jesus as word, light, healing to spiritual deafness and blindness, salvation for spiritual hunger. Despite the pessimists, renewal is becoming evident. Study groups, prayer groups, Bible seminars, ecumenical consultations and committees for pastoral care are discovered in operation over a wide spectrum of church life, bringing vigour to the community. All this means that God is being taken seriously and there is an expectancy that he will inspire thinking and empower action. It may then be possible to avoid the appalling pitfalls into which so many have tumbled. They thought they had a new gimmick for raising the money, for meeting and balancing the budget. They had not. The danger of poisoning the wells of spirituality will remain unless we all endeavour to understand what God is saying to us.

The spring of corporate responsibility

Within the parish it is the parochial church council which normally exercises corporate responsibility. The amount of time spent in PCC meetings on financial matters is an indication of the weight of the burden which problems of budget and accounts put upon its members. It rubs off on the clergy, many of whom are not at home in the mysterious columns of a balance sheet. There can be a devastating effect on that vocational certainty which issued in the promise of fulfilment after ordination. Some accept the imposed pattern of sales and subscriptions, of two major efforts a year and a constant pressure on the congregation to keep the money coming (covenanted if possible). There is no end to this and after a decade or two, the weariness of soul and sickness of heart is apparent. This is no way to conduct spiritual work. Just keeping out of debt will not release funds and energy for expansion in the parish and outside of it. That the 'show must be kept going' is inevitable, but questions must be addressed to

the way this may be done, as well as to where 'the show' is going.
Once a handful of people have learned the secret of committal
to the cause of Christ, have seen the reality of the challenge to
life in his death, and see themselves now responsible to God for
the continuance of Jesus' mission, they can revolutionize the
economics of the church they attend. This committed nucleus
must include the clergy and this may involve a lot of prayer and
tact. Then the PCC must be brought to a common mind about
new attitudes to their task and responsibilities. Some of the
nucleus will have to be personally involved as members of the
council. The same principles which have convinced individuals
about their response to God as stewards of what has been lent to
them, will apply to the budgeting and care of funds which have
been given into the hands of the PCC out of the sacrifice of
ordinary members. Stewarding the gifts of stewards is no light
responsibility and should be subject to report and accountability. One way of sharing information and giving account of
stewardship would be to turn the annual general meeting into a
lively forum for the reporting of past activities and the planning
of new ones. Behind the bare figures of what is used for what, of
what is given away for evangelism and pastoral care at home
and overseas, there are many interesting stories concerning
people and places which will stimulate the prayer life of the
congregation. World development is much to the fore. Debate
and decision on this will help with relevance and immediacy of
aid. Certainly there must be delegation, but this does not mean
that everyone else should appear to wash their hands of any
part or lot in the matter.

Christian stewardship is concerned not to serve the Church
but to serve the Lord of the Church. It is an instrument to
discover and fulfil the will of God in the growth of the kingdom.
To be exclusively concerned with the minutiae of church
regulations might well deflect the community from its real task.
The Church has to be aware of itself in a stewardship role. It
must care for its members and ought to have a great
compassion for the uncommitted mass of people outside its
fold. A house set in order is not simply to be admired, it

becomes a more efficient instrument for getting work done. Divine service is not an unimportant aspect of the Church's ministry. The worship of God must be offered worthily and everyone taking part must aim to offer the very best, whether preacher, reader, chorister, sidesman, organist or bellringer. None have any right to try to get away with the minimum effort. The work of the Lord must not be done negligently.

Whatever is undertaken by the Church should express the common devotion to Jesus by the sum of its members.

The division of England into parishes meant that everyone was within reach of a house of God and a minister of God. Times are changing and soon there will be less emphasis on the church building and little evidence of a 'priest in every parish'. Lay leaders and local ordained ministers may have much more responsibility put upon them under the direction and with the enabling of a fully trained, ordained priest. The ground can still be covered, but more and more Christians will be engaged in making contacts for God. Every town, village and hamlet is important for the people who live in it. It is part of God's vineyard, as the scriptures would put it, and must be cared for, cultivated and made productive. It does not belong to the local authority, the bishop, the rector, the squire or the PCC. It belongs to God and is committed for the time being to the care of human stewards. Their Christian concern is so to proclaim Jesus that he will be the bridge to bring souls home to God. This is the real work, and extends far beyond the immediate boundaries of the local church, however organized. Christian stewards are reminded of their commitment to Christ in his world-wide work. This affects the corporate responsibility of the PCC as well as that of the individual. The good news has to be proclaimed by faithful stewards of the unsearchable riches of Christ.

Chapter 7

Preparing for Leadership

Somehow the Church must be delivered from accepting a watered down institutional fund-raising exercise run by the institution for the institution, as Christian stewardship. This will involve some extensive theological study by those clergy and lay leaders who will be responsible for initiation. They must make up their minds about the place of the tithe and be clear about the relationship between response to the gospel and the quality of life which that inspires. Bishop Emmerich puts it thus, 'If forgiveness is the door by which we enter into the new life with God in Christ, stewardship describes the responsible attitude of that new life. If we die with Christ to selfishness, we rise with Christ to stewardship.'

The law of the tithe in the Old Testament is interpreted differently in Deuteronomy and Numbers, but in general it was the allocation of a tenth of produce mainly for the sustenance of the Levites responsible for the worship of God with a proportion for the priests. Deuteronomy includes reference to the use of the tithe not only for Levites, but for the fatherless, strangers and widows.

The book of Malachi refers to the moral depravity of a selfish society where wordly profit and self interest led to neglect of worship and a level of giving way below the prescribed tithe. Unfortunately, the blessings offered by Malachi in God's name to those who repent of the evil life and express that repentance in the acceptance of the law of the tithe, have been claimed by some Christians as the basis of an agreement with the Almighty. A quid pro quo agreement which would match blessings to a programme of tithing. No doubt blessing does come to a well ordered God-orientated life, but man cannot bargain with God.

In the New Testament, Christ is scathing about the way the lawyers and Pharisees give a tenth even of the herbs, but leave aside justice, mercy and honesty. When legalism takes over it darkens human perception and destroys the freedom of the human spirit.

A modern view of the tithe

In our own time, much that was covered by the charitable use of the tithe is taken care of by the taxes imposed by a government. The sick, the unemployed, the elderly, the disabled are relieved from begging by the redistribution of money from the better off. Thus the tithe cannot be transplanted from an ancient agrarian economy into the procedures of today. But its spirit can; the tithe would sanctify the whole and had to be offered in a worshipful and thankful spirit to the glory of God. That can still be done if the tenth is taken as a starting point for thought and prayer. The very wealthy would be free to give much more. Some, who are comfortably off even after tax, may find it possible to allocate a tenth for God and general benevolence. The great majority might find the tenth too much after meeting their minimum obligations and would come to a figure proportionate to their capital or their income in the giving of which they would feel neither pride nor shame. That figure on those calculations would be a right figure. It would have no permanent significance but would have to be reviewed at every change of circumstance. Stewardship is not a financial strait-jacket. It represents freedom to use personal initiative in the care of what ultimately belongs to the master.

Dealing with wealth

In the New Testament there is no authority for any particular way of dealing with wealth. There is no presumption for renunciation or of common ownership. Incidents involving Jesus support a variety of possibilities.

1. Everything may be given to the poor.
2. Half to be given away and a fourfold repayment of fraud.
3. Lend and expect nothing back.
4. A little with love is greater than a lot which has little effect on what is left.
5. The apparently foolish prodigality of a broken jar of ointment must not be evaluated.
6. Some service must involve money, but other is immediate and personal. The hungry, thirsty, sick, strangers and prisoners may need money or what money can buy, but caring hospitality and visiting is more demanding on time and personal availability. Taking time off for a funeral may even be included.

Those called to leadership must have more than a nodding acquaintance with the facts of the Gospels and the Christian way of life which lies behind the writing of the Epistles. Modern man has proudly accepted the proposition that he has come of age. The advance in knowledge and technique has been staggering but there has been no corresponding increase of personal satisfaction. The tensions of existence are as painful as ever. Man seems to be obscured by clouds of frustration. If he is to be confronted with the offer of the gospel, he must first be found.

Human beings do not all look alike and though there may be several ways of general classification, individuality remains. Not all have the same level of intellectual understanding. New thought, new organization, changed circumstances and revolution do not find the same general reaction. Without God there is little light on the human condition and none that would give it an optimistic outlook. When God came to man, he came where he was and through the human life of Jesus spoke relevantly to his condition. We are commissioned to do the same.

Any stewardship programme must be so deeply related to the gospel that it becomes an address to the whole person. He is a social being, a family man, a worker, one who handles money and has some political sense. He is also a child of God and theologically in the category 'sinner'. There has been a break between creature and creator. The creature has lost his way and lives with an inner question, 'How can I find God?'

Relating fact to experience

He should be encouraged to start with the elementary facts. Jesus existed, died by crucifixion, after which 'something happened' and a body of followers were knit together into a Church. By witness and the ministry of preaching, teaching, healing and contending with evil Christianity grew. In this religion the suffering and death of Jesus was not presented as defeat and disaster but as power and sovereignty. Suffering and the power are linked together. The cross and the glory go together, not only for Jesus, but for those who live this truth. The triumph comes through in their teaching, in their manner of life, their ethical stance and in their experience. Something happened to link the cross with the glory. Either that happening was a great illusion or the resurrection of Jesus. The gloom of Good Friday indicates that the disciples had not understood and were baffled. By Easter day the revolution was complete. The significance of resurrection linked past with present and guaranteed a future bliss in the company of the Lord. This 'die to live' experience of Jesus became the pattern of life for his followers, invited to die to self and to inherit eternal life. God presents himself in Christ to the 'now' of every life, sharing and transforming, calling to the commitment of fellowship with him, which gives freedom, uses suffering and proclaims a meaningful and coherent universe. So Jesus is placarded as the epitome of the divine authority.

Stewardship mission continues in its own particular way the work begun by Jesus and committed to his disciples. He came preaching the gospel of the kingdom of God to which he linked a call to a change of mind. People have to make up their minds about him and to accept him as king in the new kingdom. The new teaching is based upon himself. People are near the kingdom or far from it as they react to the person of the king. The kingdom parables provide light on several aspects, the nature of the king, the nature of the kingdom, the character of its subjects, and the manner of its growth.

Training for leadership
Mark's Gospel provides a good agenda for the training of disciples.

1. They are not simply the recipients of teaching, they are involved with Jesus in the apostolic task.
2. He will discover their skills and use them. Those Galileans are to become fishers of men.
3. The teaching is to be no academic exercise, it is to express itself in active care and concern.
4. In the early stages Jesus does all the work and his disciples look on, getting accustomed to the new power and authority which communicates and heals.
5. They are introduced to the conception of co-operating faith which accelerates the process. They see new light cast on the sabbath as good for man, and not just good in itself.
6. After their probation, retreat into the hill country results in the call and commission of the twelve.
7. They are to be with him and he is to send them to preach, heal and overcome evil.
8. The first tentative steps are taken in pairs.
9. They listen to more teaching, watch a practical demonstration in compassion and aid and listen to an argument with the legalists.
10. They learn that method is flexible, nothing is mere repetition.

Watching the development of the disciples we discern their being moulded on the model of the new humanity. They learn that status, position and ability are not matters for arrogance or pride, all selfishness must be denied and the childlike character coveted. They are caught up in the dramatic events of Calvary and the last days and are much perplexed thereby. The story of the disciples' part in that drama makes unhappy reading. The anxious atmosphere of the upper room is heightened by the exit into darkness of the misguided traitor. Peter fails through fear, and cowardice drives the others away too. Something binds the disciples together and soon they are meeting behind locked doors, still bewildered, still trying to relate what they had been taught to what they now experience. Then they saw Jesus, and on the third day they were sure. Seven weeks of presence and prayer prepare them for the parting. No longer will they imitate the master, they will act as fellow workers possessed by the same Spirit. Pupils no longer, they pass out to exercise a total ministry and numbers are added to the Church.

Bringing out the meaning
St Paul, after his conversion, struggled to compare and evaluate the new teaching and to think through the implications of resurrection for humanity. He does not repeat Jesus' preaching of the kingdom, because for him, the good news is Jesus himself. Salvation is made available by Jesus' death on a cross. His resurrection validates faith and preaching. Christianity is a universal religion, not a Jewish sect. Faith is a living activity by which anyone may respond to the message and become incorporated into the people of God. 'The gospel is the saving power of God for everyone who has faith' (Romans 1.16). The searching and finding of a man in his actual situation is God's own act. We may pray, witness, work or argue but the Holy Spirit converts. The past is dealt with, the present is acceptable and the future loses its paralysing power of intimidation. Nothing shall separate us from the love of God.

By attention to Jesus we learn fundamental truths about the love of God and the condition of the human race. By attention to St Paul we can see the application of the benefits of the gospel in the day-to-day battle against temptation and in the excitement of a spiritual pilgrimage. By attention to both, we learn what it means to be a leader.

There have been periods in the Church's history when a great concern with internal organization inhibited a world view. The longing for solidarity provided material for the heresy struggles of the early centuries and left the church divided. More recently the search for a new unity has broken down many barriers. The church is discovering a new stewardship of itself as an instrument in the hand of God.

Without a firm grasp on the theological basis of humanity's relation to God, those who would lead in any kind of stewardship activity will be ineffective. Without the constraints and guidelines of a real grasp of the concept of stewardship, the result will be a flimsy version of an envelope scheme. When motivation is wrong the individual gets depressed and the parish apathetic.

Chapter 8

Finding out
What People Think

One of the facts which emerged from a survey of methods used in the dioceses, was the endeavour, on the part of promoters of stewardship schemes, to find out what ordinary church people thought of the place of their parish church in their own esteem, and in relation to the community in which it was set. There is little hope of new teaching being accepted if it seems to contradict firmly held views. A study to discover what people really think must usually be conducted in an anonymous manner so that views can be expressed with no fear of contradiction or ridicule. Of course, a great deal of prejudice and some measure of nonsense will emerge, but patient persistence may lead from a quick analysis of things as they are to the development of a thoughtful long term plan. The completion of a questionnaire is one of the easiest ways to explore the thinking of a group of people. The questions can range from the general, which ask for an overall assessment of church life, to the particular, which go into detail about aspects of parish organization and planning as well as personal questions about prayer, Bible reading and interest in the welfare of others. This pursuit of knowledge must guarantee anonymity to those who take part in order to give honesty the widest scope and to protect the outspoken from reprisals from threatened authority.

An attitude study

The study of people's attitudes and prejudices can form a good basis of group discussion. The comments of individuals can be fed into the group and something near the truth will emerge in the findings. Opposite ideas from the camps of failure or of success can challenge inquiring minds to discover what is the truth. Inevitably worship will come under scrutiny. The clergy as leaders in liturgy may find that their voices could be improved. The choir and organist will hear a variety of things about themselves which could help in the kind of approach made to music and song, which bears on the quality of worship and its appeal to the occasional visitor. Clergy may be encouraged to learn that their sermons are the right length, but disturbed that their content is poor and their delivery confusing. But taken in good part, to discover what people think can be a profitable exercise.

The questions should not however stop at the ready made Aunt Sally of the parish establishment. Individuals should be asked for:

1. an honest assessment of their own prayer life;
2. how often they read the Bible;
3. what time they give to study the Bible;
4. whether they make use of the bookstall and read Christian literature;
5. what are their feelings of responsibility for their neighbours;
6. whether they are engaged in some project of community aid.

Answers will reveal whether the neighbourhood and other churches have any impact on the thinking of the person in the pew. Besides exploring the pastoral challenge, it is an advantage to open up on the evangelistic opportunity presented in youth work, adult education and confirmation preparation. One of the encouraging signs culled from information submitted by dioceses and stewardship agencies has been the number of adults offering themselves for confirmation.

Challenged to grow
Discussion stimulated by the collation of opinions expressed by most of a congregation should not terminate in words. Change will be indicated as needed in the corporate life of the parish as well as in the life style of individuals. There are many among us who dislike change so deeply that they will oppose it, as they would say, 'on principle and even if it is for the better'. Such people have to be treated with loving care, but should not be allowed to veto what may well be the pressure of the Holy Spirit towards a more realistic pursuit of the characteristics of the kingdom of God. There is little point in raising income or of dedicating time and talents for the maintenance of a status quo, or just to keep the show going. The Church exists for those outside it; and all discussion, prayer, effort and devoted giving must spring from a desire to fulfil the will of God for his fellow workers. Without them the mission of Jesus makes little headway, and may even hinder or inhibit response from thoughtful onlookers. Church history is full of examples of the ill effects of self preservation or self-aggrandizement.

People want to be effective
Experience indicates that our church people do want to take their religion seriously, and time and time again there is a plea for teaching and for help with community care. It would be a disgrace if it were still true that 'the hungry sheep look up, and are not fed'. A church which is inward looking, concerned only for its institutional stability will quickly give the impression that it is only people's money that it is after—a fatal flaw in thoughtless fundraising.

Finding out what people think will provide plenty of material for constructive teaching, the correction of error and prejudice and occasionally the 'driving out of heresy'. Positively, the encouragement to worship the real God and to serve him for Jesus' sake will sharpen witness and deepen devotion.

It may be of help if the areas of enquiry are indicated. The

questions have to be specific to reveal the personal attitude to
the subjects suggested. It must be borne in mind that any
endeavour to reach an assessment of a person's own particular
view of any subject will be compromised, even rendered useless,
if what is intended to be a personal probe should become the
basis of a general discussion. Some people have alarming
powers of manipulation! A personal study of individual
attitudes should be kept to the individual and should be
guaranteed anonymity. By this means even the most timid and
conformist will be free to express praise or criticism without
fear or favour. After all, it is the truth we pursue and we may
expect a properly mounted study of attitudes, prayerfully
prepared, to lead to a spring-board of consensus.

Areas of enquiry

(a) To begin with, there should be questions about the way the
Church is accepting the commission to make disciples. Try to
reach people's experience in this area, rather than ask for
theory. What approach and methods actually work for them.
(b) Then discover what people think of any corporate outreach
in which the church is engaged and whether the life of the
church and the congregation has any evangelistic impact.
(c) There is an ongoing discussion about the effectiveness of
church worship. Minds have to be lifted beyond the 1662/ASB
preferences to questions about the reason why so many people
avoid any kind of commitment to the regular worship of God.
(d) Congregations constantly request help from the clergy in
the matter of prayer. Discover the basic belief about prayer
which people hold. Find out the areas of difficulty and assess
the scope and depth of prayer experience.
(e) Similar questions should be used to assess:

  (i) what is the attitude to the Bible;
  (ii) how much is it studied;
  (iii) how often read.

Be prepared for disappointments in these areas.

It is valuable to discover how closely a congregation is in touch with world Christian news:

(a) Do they read church newspapers?

(b) Are they conversant with missionary societies' newsletters and literature?

(c) Every church should have a bookstall. Discover how much it is appreciated and how greatly used. Challenge about the relevance of Christian faith can bring interesting comments about its impact on the family and on work, profession, office or school. The church ought to have something to say about social issues, how far should involvement go? Specific problems in society should be identified and a declaration of personal interest invited.

(d) No study would be complete which did nothing to elucidate various attitudes to money and possessions. Prejudice believes that the church is always asking for money; realism knows that money cannot be excluded, but what is the person's attitude to Christian giving.

(e) Church life in general provides an area for assessment. Many churches provide clubs and activities for every conceivable group. Others are accused of neglect of youth or of the older people. In some the clergy 'do everything', in others there is a lively conception of lay ministry. Search for the ideal will produce criticism of the present state and some good ideas.

The ecumenical debate

Finally it would be well to open up the ecumenical debate to find out how real and pressing is the search for the 'coming great Church'.

The two vitally important matters concerning the use of questionnaires are anonymity and outside assessment. People will not fill in any form which requires an honest, no holds barred, approach if there is the slightest possibility of its authorship being discovered. Then . . .

> if the analysis and assessment of the forms is to be effective, it must be done by an independent third

party. Anyone closely identified with the answering group would almost unconsciously suppress or play down unpleasant details and overemphasize the signs of success. Better leave the assessment to an unrelated expert, free from the constraints of censorship.

Chapter 9

Training Visitors

To anyone unused to calling on others, the prospect of enrolling as a visitor is a daunting business and many hold back. Often the first reactions can be overcome by a promise that visitors will be properly trained. The promise indicates that visiting is a responsible and worthwhile activity which should not be undertaken lightly and may be easily ruined by incompetent amateurism.

Those who are enrolled as potential visitors in a stewardship project should be clear first of all about their own personal commitment as God's stewards. They will have expressed that commitment, not only by volunteering as visitors, but also by making a meaningful, proportionate and generous financial promise.

There are, it will transpire, a variety of methods of conducting a stewardship project, but in all of them the role of the visitor is crucial. Untrained visitors who are sent off with a list, to make contact in their own ways as best they may, will have a baneful effect upon the ultimate outcome.

The number of training sessions varies, but generally there are at least three, called for a time convenient for all the visitors. It is essential that every visitor should attend every session. During each of these there should be adequate time for prayer, instruction and questions. Questions should be encouraged, so that answers may be offered in areas causing concern to those who have to go out alone into the parish. When visitors feel that they have had adequate training, the Sunday commissioning becomes an exciting occasion of identification with God's plan as his fellow workers.

The attitude to the task must be right. Visitors are not professional beggars on behalf of God or his Church. Nor are they out to sell something. The commercial aspects of the dealings of church-people with the community is not easy to erase, since it has been in such constant use. The basis of fair exchange of goods for money may entertain addicted 'shoppers' but it has little to do with the making of new Christians. In one sense, the visitor's approach ought not to fall into the category of the distribution of gifts. People are now very suspicious of the free gift and immediately suspect 'a catch in it somewhere'.

Rather, the visitor has something to share. He wants to share the treasure of his knowledge of Christ, his enjoyment of the fellowship of the church and his calling to use himself and his resources for God and general benevolence. He will not feel competent to cover that agenda in one meeting, but he can discuss some aspect of the stewardship project and offer an invitation to join in what is planned. The person visited should be someone with a recognizable link with the church. It is always best to proceed on the basis of a man's own assessment of himself as a churchman. Others may feel that he is further off than he thinks, but it is upon his assessment and not theirs that a visitor must proceed. It is possible to advance from where he thinks he is to a more positive and committed place in the church of God.

Each visit matters

The visitor is about the master's business. That is rather like a farmer checking his stock or a shepherd counting and caring for his sheep. Jesus described himself as a shepherd and taught the importance of the individual and his value, even when wayward and a cause of anxiety and trouble. Each one should receive the same sacrificial dedication of labour and time, despite waywardness and an eye ever lifted to the neighbour's field where the grass is always greener, despite too the rather dull sameness of a flock of sheep. Our people are not there to be fleeced or devoured—even for their own good!

Visitation is an expression of care, which must not be narrow and exclusive, nor fussy and dominating. The eastern shepherd went ahead to point the way, but had an eye for the weak and the lame. The care expressed is of the Church who sends the visitor, and of the Lord of the Church whose character is an open handed providence clearly demonstrated in Jesus. So the visitor, knowing who and what he represents has to develop his own awareness of areas where he might encourage, and others where he might offer specific help. The quiet and cool approach is so much better than boisterous 'doing of good'.

The visitor must know his limitations. He is not a social worker (unless trained for it). He is not a marriage guidance counsellor, nor an expert in child guidance. He is a caring Christian offering a share in friendship, and in the secrets of the spiritual life.

Before a visitor sets out he should take a few minutes for recollection and prayer—to remind himself of his special commission, to make a friendly contact to open the way for the Holy Spirit to act. The old promise to Joshua is valid today, 'Be strong and of good courage, do not be afraid....' The memory of this will avert the panic which wants to pray, on approaching a forbidding front door, 'Dear God, may they be out'. Be sure you have the names right, not simply on a card but in your mind. Be sure that it will be a convenient time—World Cup has a large television audience. Television is not such an obstacle now as in the early days. It is relatively easy to identify the rubbish when polite hosts will turn the machine off. If the visitor has any prejudices about the family he is visiting, he should leave them behind. The only important factor is God's interest in them and his love for them.

The basis of a good visit is proper conversation. The visitor may be a splendid lecturer, but that skill is out of place here. Let the people talk; find out what they think and help them to enjoy the visit. This is good for the visitor as well and will reduce any unnecessary level of nervousness. Criticism of vicar, church

people or church services may be offered. The best way to
handle this is the humble approach which reckons no one is
perfect, and asks what they suggest for remedies. The way to
disaster is to fly into a 'rage of defence'—which will confirm
them in their criticism and break off all useful contact. So
argument should be avoided; there is no profit in winning an
argument and losing a potential friend. Sometimes the visitor
will be asked a question which completely floors him. An
honest regret that he does not know the answer will be
respected, and he can promise to find out and will call again.

We are not all called to be evangelists, but we are all able to
say what the Lord Christ means to us and to speak about
church life and daily life lived by the help of God. The visitor
must not be a religious bore or a maniac who attacks everyone
else in order to prove himself right. Transubstantiation and
predestination are probably topics best avoided. To be able to
speak of one's personal faith when this is required is a quiet and
effective way of witness.

A master plan
The visitation requires planning and will involve others besides
the visitors in setting it up. It should not seem to be a secret
operation. The plan, once prepared should be made known in
the parish magazine or newsletter and in special stewardship
literature. The calls upon the houses of parishioners when they
come must be expected—visitors should be supplied with a card
giving the fullest information about the family to be visited. The
names and occupations, whether in work or not; it is important
to get it right. People are sensitive about themselves and resent
any slur on their identity. They matter to themselves and must
matter to those who call.

Calls may be made by appointment; there can be a degree of
informality about these arrangements which can be agreed on
the street or in a pub. If a call is made 'on the off chance' and the
folk are out, this means another call at some other time. Putting
paper through a letter box is not a call, makes no contact and
will probably produce no result.

The relaxed visitor will make a good impression if it is natural for him to use a smile when he is greeting anyone. If it is not natural he must work at it until it is. Thinking about the Lord more often and being thankful for his blessings lifts the spirits and tones up the muscles used in the smile. The aim must be to convey relaxation and to put the persons visited at their ease.

The question of confidentiality must be faced. It must be assumed that everything said by the family during a visit is said as to a friend who will not gossip. If any matter ought to be passed on to the vicar or some other person, permission must be asked first. This should not present too much of a problem to visitors, but they must be wise. It is so important to develop mutual trust. The reason for a regular pattern of visiting over a long period is for people to get to know one another. In time of crisis the visitor will be a person to whom the needy may turn.

A visitor will need the qualities of patience and tolerance if he is to be acceptable. He must avoid emotional involvement and adopt a professional attitude of detachment. It is facile and naive to suppose that being a Christian will protect from all accident and consequences of frailty; or that all problems can be solved to the comfort and satisfaction of faithful disciples. Jesus did not avoid the cross; St Paul had to accept the thorn in the flesh: faith enables us to live with our ongoing problems. Visitors must be aware then of the temptations to give too much advice and to do too much themselves. A sense of humour and the capacity for listening are safeguards against arrogance.

Chapter 10

Problems! What about Time and Talents

Some promoters of Christian stewardship projects are fearful that the money aspect will be too obtrusive, and unless carefully handled this leads to an unbalanced approach. On the one hand, money is relegated to such an unimportant position that the financial return from the special effort is extremely disappointing. On the other hand, to inflate the importance of a response in the field of time and talents will sometimes bring an embarrassingly large number of offers so that some people are unable to be employed.

Since the challenge of Christian stewardship is to the whole person it is obvious that our time and our talents must form some part of our response, just as the need for a financial commitment cannot be omitted. A very high proportion of the breadwinner's time, as also of the time of the housekeeper, is taken up with daily work. It is in this field that the Christian has to be sure that what he does, and the manner of its performance, represents his Christian commitment and raises no question of any double standard in his lifestyle. Bad workmanship and slack management are a misuse of talent and a cynical waste of time, especially for the Christian. The witness of the steward is best shown in his daily contacts; then if there is time to spare after proper care for family and home demands, he can be available for community care projects and church maintenance.

Preparing long lists of jobs needing to be done demands a great deal of research and the end result may well be an embarrassment of riches in only a small proportion on the list. The other jobs do not get done, and some who have offered cannot be used. Would it not be better to divorce time and talent lists from stewardship projects and concentrate on the challenge to the individual to be available as need is identified, and to express his devotion by a worthy promise in financial terms?

There is danger, too, in going to another extreme. Some would drop every challenge to personal response other than the financial one. This means that those approached can only hear 'it is your money we are after'. By this means a stewardship project slips into a fund-raising exercise with consequent loss of momentum once the period of the campaign is over; and a similar intensive drive has to be mounted a few years later.

The better plan is for a thoughtful piece of literature to be produced which can be the agenda for a teaching seminar, and also a set of guidelines about the way in which time and natural abilities can be used all the time as an expression of Christian faith. Study the agenda for a weekend workshop in the Appendix.

Community projects and missionary endeavour

In researching for this book, many exciting community projects came to light and a sample scheme which was designed to do something, however small, to help in the third world has gripped the imagination. Time and enthusiastic interest from a group of Christians can give them personal satisfaction and do something about the comment of Jesus, 'The poor you have always with you'.

One of the most inhibiting things to the wider view of Christian responsibility is the feeling that so much needs to be done about maintaining the local church that there is no chance to look outside.

The missionary endeavour of a past age, which gripped the imagination of Christians longing to win a world for Christ, has diminished to such an extent that missionary interest seems to be now confined to a small minority who keep in touch with a society or an individual working in some foreign part of the world. Others take note of the challenge of foreign cultures in our own country and endeavour to establish a bridgehead with the immigrant population. In this case too it is less an interest of the whole church than for the few who take it aboard as an optional extra. In a situation where the indigenous population is apathetic and where there is a noticeable minority of incomers, there can be no excuse for the church to close its eyes to the need to make more Christians. The so called 'mission field' may seem remote and Victorian methods of evangelism be regarded with disfavour, but the fields are as ripe for harvest as ever they were and new ways of contact must be explored. Some parishes have been stimulated in their thinking and in their response to the challenges of stewardship by the tragic situation in the underdeveloped parts of the world, brought to our notice by the *Brandt Report* and *Common Crisis*. An example of a parish involvement in a scheme of aid is the trust set up by the parish of St Mark, Reigate. The scheme was started in 1979 as a result of church members seeing the film *Five minutes to midnight* which is about deprivation in the third world. It followed the pattern of an organization set up a few years earlier in Salford with the intention of doing something, however small to alleviate suffering in underdeveloped countries. One of the trustees had a link with Lesotho and the first project was to bring water to enable the villagers to grow vegetables as a self help effort to fight malnutrition. Parishioners were asked to imagine entertaining a guest for Christmas from a third world country and to give the cost of that to establish a fund.

From then the scheme has never lacked support and besides the pioneer project in Lesotho a number of projects have been carried out in Africa, in Bangladesh and in Trinidad. Here is the sort of imaginative co-operative stewardship programme which can combine the individual gifts for general benevolence with a parochial church council allocation for the work of God abroad. The trust has moved away from simply giving financial aid, into helping the underprivileged to find the means to survive by their own efforts. Now, where it is not possible to provide private agents for projects, adequate advice is available from the larger agencies like Oxfam or Christian Aid. The trust idea is spreading and has the effect of linking the stewardship of money to an identifiable project, and is a witness to those who will heed, that Christian stewardship is not only concerned with support for the local church.

When Christian stewardship gained momentum in Australia, the allocation from the top of the pile for God and general benevolence was seen as a great trust fund held by an unlimited number of trustees who could arrange for money to be allocated to any particular area of expansion or need in the work of God's kingdom. A youth club in Britain once rejoiced in the gift of table tennis equipment from one such trustee.

Stewardship covers a very wide field. Not only are decisions made about the allocation of capital and income, but also in specific projects where money can be an agent and a power to get things done.

Chapter 11

Project Methods

The author's thanks and appreciation go to those executive officers in many dioceses who answered questions on behalf of their bishops about the stewardship situation in the diocese. Their replies covered activity which ranged from simple fund-raising by projects directed widely in the community and beyond the church family, through schemes whose main thrust was to channel direct giving into a widespread acceptance of covenanting, to the kind of effort which warranted the use of the word 'mission' as a description of basic intent. Financially the fund-raising schemes gave better than average results in the initial year, especially when promises were supported by the signing of a form of covenant. Some parishes would seem to have had no difficulty in accepting the advice of the Reverend George F. Regan of the Episcopal Church of the United States of America, quoted in Redmond Mullin's recent book *The Wealth of Christians* (Paternoster Press). Fr Regan links stewardship and fund-raising and says, 'the best way to do both ... is through a personal witness in the home. With candour a layperson shares what is happening to him or to her.' 'This is what I am giving; this is why I am giving it; this is what it has meant to my life. . . .'

Such a direct and forthright approach is not universally acceptable. The challenge has to be made nevertheless and it is here that there is a great deal of variety. Some rely upon the briefing of visitors, others on publicity from magazine or pulpit, others by the publication of the total promises of the inner core of workers. If there is evidence of generous response the impact is expected to be sufficient to inspire thoughtful, honest and prayerful consideration of any personal financial promise.

Some congregations do not feel that it is appropriate to mount any kind of scheme and rely upon an acceptance of a literal interpretation of the principle of tithing. Whatever the temptations may be to complacency and spiritual self satisfaction, the result in charitable giving and missionary support cannot but be commended.

The Adisham initiative
Stewardship in some dioceses has lately been revived by the infusion of new blood and a revised presentation. In Canterbury, for instance, the Archbishop's sermon at a parish stewardship commissioning of visitors at Adisham was printed and distributed to every parish in the diocese for discussion and action. In the course of his sermon, the Archbishop spoke about the meaning and practice of Christian stewardship. 'Christian stewardship ... is about every department of a Christian life. It is about our need first to respond with thanks to God for all his blessings and then to offer God through Jesus Christ our souls and bodies to be a living sacrifice. This is a basic human instinct. Someone once said there are two ways of looking at life: you can take it for granted or you can take it with gratitude and the choice you make determines your character. ... Thanksgiving for what God has given us in life and for what God has done for us through Jesus Christ is a starting point.' Pointing out that stewardship is very different from fund-raising, the Archbishop nevertheless underlined the importance of money by referring to the parable of the talents. 'I think (Jesus) also meant us to take the money part of it literally. Will not God call us to account for what we have done with our money?'

That sermon was preached at the service which marked the beginning of a stewardship mission in the parish of Adisham, but it also marked the beginning of a new diocesan stewardship effort. This operation became known as 'the Adisham Initiative' and produced a maximum work load for the stewardship adviser. To cope with the work a team of honorary advisers is being built up. Their training, of course, puts an extra responsbility upon the adviser. The time spent in preparation for what is increasingly being called a parish stewardship mission is lengthening. It may well begin with a weekend workshop, drawing together leaders from several parishes considering the possibilities and wanting to learn how it should be done. Since a general acceptance of a proper level of regular giving ought not to be the end of the exercise, but a means to deeper commitment, the subject of a parish plan takes an important place on the agenda. Teaching and training of congregation and visitors is spread over a longer period than 'the short sharp shock' of twenty-five years ago. Nevertheless, the intensive phase is not protracted and a well prepared administration and visiting programme leads to smooth operation.

A west country experiment

The special programme worked out with the full involvement of the Bishop in the diocese of Bath and Wells under the title of 'the Standard', reached a climax in 1980. In that year a diocesan-wide visitation of parochial church councils was undertaken by specially trained and commissioned lay visitors. The ongoing teaching of a five per cent standard of giving has been guided by a small group of clergy and lay people presided over by a bishop's chaplain who was also an incumbent. The fifth Sunday before Christmas was designated Diocesan Commitment Sunday. The main vehicle of communication is through a newsletter which ranges widely over the field of Christian activity. From 1984 there was to be a review of the project and those concerned would be looking for areas for development and improvement in the mobilization and use of resources.

Pressure from the quota

It is clear from many returns that great pressure has been put upon parishes because of increased diocesan quotas to meet the ravages of inflation and the increases in stipends and maintenance costs. The Church Commissioners are unable to maintain a high percentage of grant towards these needs and consequently look to the people in the pew to meet any shortfall. The policy of some dioceses is to give the fullest information about the money required to run the diocese. Some by diagrams indicate how much of the cake has to be supplied by parishes. Boards of finance feel themselves forced to this approach because of their responsibility to balance the budget, and the stewardship department is used to put the needs across. This way of thinking and working has always caused difficulties for churchmen who feel instinctively that giving to God ought not to be dominated by the needs of the institution. Targets tend to reduce the level of generous giving, because they are usually set within the compass of 'church supporters' and not 'Christian givers'. Financiers' arguments are always plausible, can be put forward under the shadow of approaching disaster and lead to a panic response. Faith believes that the resources are there, devotion will release them more readily than pressure.

A very important point which emerges is the personal involvement of so many diocesan bishops in stewardship planning in their dioceses. It was not ever so; and the unhappiness of advisers in the early years reflected their isolation in a work then considered to be peripheral to traditional diocesan activity. In a report to the Archbishop of Canterbury after a visit to Australia and New Zealand in 1976 the following appears: 'There must be leadership given from the highest levels. Those dioceses which were moving into an area of greater freedom about money were dioceses where the bishop had taken the initiative and with a strong lead had brought his people into the exercise.'

There was of course the disappointment if, after the lead was given, select parishes could not follow!

There is evidence that the traditional three-year programme is still followed. Usually this involves a parish gathering of some kind with a self catering supper or modest dinner and visits to parishioners from a hostess and another trained person whose responsibility is to collect promise cards. One reported scheme involved a large effort and extensive visitation every five years and no other approach in the intervening years. Some relate to four year covenant periods, with an annual stewardship Sunday in the intervening years.

Much of the promotion of stewardship has a strong emphasis on commitment. The foundation is the call for a response to the gift of Christ to die for humanity. The financial aspect is firmly held in the area of response for 'after all, the Church is not in business to make ends meet. Its job is to make disciples of Christ—to reach out in mission.' This is a quotation from a diocesan leaflet, and is typical of a lot of material springing from an endeavour to see stewardship as part of Christian living.

On the other hand, another adviser saw 1983 as an important year for his department, educating and explaining to parishes the problems with which the diocese was faced financially. To get to a realistic appreciation of the role the laity have to play was the aim, in order that the church should not be 'bugged' perpetually by money matters. This programme developed a growing understanding of the type of help required, and it was gratifying to the adviser to note that this did not appear to be solely confined to an increase in giving.

Team parishes and groups of parishes produce their own advantages and problems when endeavouring to do a project together. The experience of one parish in the team or group opting out is not uncommon and causes an unnecessary strain on relationships in the early stages and difficulties about how to incorporate them later after a change of mind. For usually the benefit seen to accrue to parish life by making stewardship part of the normal life of a congregation, is perfectly apparent, and makes its own quiet demand for attention.

Problems caused by opting out

The attitude of non-co-operation is an extension of what all parishes still have to contend with among members of the congregation. There are those who will not come in. They must not be abandoned, nor must their attitude be allowed to depress the enthusiasm of the majority. It is a long term task facing clergy and lay leaders, to work at the problem in order to discover some acceptable local approach which will enable them to penetrate the thinking of the dissidents. Their numbers are not neglible, ranging as high as *fifty-two per cent* of those whose church affiliation ought to have resulted in positive response. In one report there was a sad note that even some PCC members were unable to take part. We must not lose heart over such a heavy barrage of resistance. Everyone who was involved in stewardship mission from the earliest days in the 1950s will remember how formidable the task was then. Great strides have been made in the presentation of the principles of stewardship and in the success of persuading doubtful people to accept them. An average of *thirty-five per cent*, over the country, who will not come in presents a challenge to our patience, our persistence and our love for them. Those who know that stewardship helps to maintain a good and satisfying lifestyle, full of spiritual potential, will not hold back from endeavouring to share such a treasure. The day when we disband our stewardship departments is a long way off. We cannot relax into a joyful acceptance that stewardship is part of the ongoing life of every church and the basis of living for every Christian – that must remain our aim.

Reports show a general rise in personal giving from the 1983 statistic of 77 pence as an average weekly offering from church members. A great deal of discussion has gone on about the accuracy of this figure. Some say, 'It must be more', others, 'It could be less'. Perhaps we should settle for its acceptance as the best that available figures could do. It is not difficult for any stewardship project, which includes basic teaching and a challenge to a prayerful response, to move ahead of that lamentable average. But we have a long way to go to get out of the grip of coin-controlled giving. People who take the tithe seriously have their sights raised, and their thoughtfulness is reflected in the generosity of their giving. There can be a meanness in contributing to the upkeep of the local church to the exclusion of all other causes, many of which relate very closely to the affairs of the kingdom of God. The greater understanding of the care of our heavenly Father and the self giving of Jesus beyond the limit, delivers from a legalistic calculated gift into the freedom of generosity.

Advantage of covenanting

It is the act of a wise man to ensure that his gift should have the maximum value. So the advantages offered by government in stimulating charitable giving by means of tax related covenant should be taken seriously. There is plenty of literature on the subject of the seven year covenant and of the more recently introduced four year covenant. Dealing with covenants, however, should be one stage beyond the decision about the size of the gift. That is the crucial decision and any bonus from the taxman does not enter into it.

Variation in method and direction

The procedure for signing a covenant is simple and the benefits highly desirable. The responsibility for reclaiming the tax from the Inland Revenue lies with the PCC acting through its treasurer. Mowbray's *A Handbook of Parish Finance*—pages 85 to 94—offers a great deal of expert help over the operation of covenants.

From the information available it appears that stewardship activity in the dioceses falls into four main divisions:

1. The traditional three year cycle of campaigns, with variations of four years or five years.
2. The covenant based comprehensive canvas with a review at the end of the period.
3. A stewardship mission based on a teaching and study programme in house groups and conferences.

4. Thanksgiving linked with pastoral care, involving
   a challenge to sacrificial giving and a commitment
   to regular visiting of five families.

There are many variations and the advisers endeavour to match
a programme to the particular needs of a parish. Some separate
the financial challenge from the approach for offers of skills in
time and talent. Others provide all the workers needed for a 'do
it yourself' effort, assisted by the adviser in the necessary
training.

   Direction of campaigns varies as well. Some advisers,
because they are unable to meet all requests, have a training
programme to enable lay people to supervise a parish project.
Visiting in the early days of stewardship campaigns put a great
strain upon a limited number of men. In those pioneering days
it was reckoned that the church's image was best presented by
men. Now we are more concerned with reality than with image,
and the welcome rescue from work and frustration has come
from the noble band of women who have shared the task with
marvellous feminine enthusiasm. The trend away from the
formidable list of people to be visited, down to a reasonable
number of about five, means that there can be proper,
unhurried sharing of conversation in a visit which should be the
forerunner of many more regular calls. Though there are still
traces of 'postal publicity' the vast majority of stewardship
programmes are based on face-to-face visitation. Some are so
convinced of the value of this that visiting becomes part of the
normal life of a church, and a permanent band of visitors is kept
in being to maintain a regular scheme of visiting, offering a
pastoral oversight which is an inherent part of all ministry.

Get good advice
There is a great deal of advice now available to any incumbent,
parochial church council or steering committee desirous of
embarking on a programme of teaching and challenge to
commitment. It is well to consult as widely as possible so as to
avoid the pitfalls and threat of disaster which ill conceived self
effort seems to invite. The whole subject is bedevilled by

prejudice and misunderstanding and all engaged in it must know the answers before the questions are asked. To imagine that the mounting of a project is a simple matter is to go into a March gale clad in tissue paper.

Get advice, therefore, and be sure it is good advice. There is now enough experience of success and failure to ensure that, taking the peculiarities of any parish into account, the matching of giving to devotion will mean the release of adequate resources for doing the will of God in basic kingdom extension and the shepherding of the faithful. Whims of vicars, organists and pressure groups will be kept in check by God's provision, through the response of his people, of what is needful.

What sort of questions should you pose to yourselves before you seek any advice from a third party?

1. Does he understand the difference between Christian stewardship and fund-raising?
2. Does he see the need for a programme of education?
3. Does he see that visitors need training and briefing?
4. What part will money play in this project? Will it be depressed in importance; will it dominate; or will it be realistic?
5. How will decisions about those to be involved be arrived at?
6. What sort of continual oversight during the project will be available?
7. What organization will be necessary to cover the work?
8. How will the follow-up be organized so that momentum is not lost?

Anyone who is to advise and help needs to have arrived himself. He needs to be committed to Christ, including sacrificial giving in financial terms. To mean well is not good enough for any of us who should be effective fellow workers with God.

There is a reference to stewardship schemes in Mowbray's *A*

Handbook of Parish Finance: 'Some parishes opt for an entirely "do it yourself" scheme. This is not to be recommended. A deal of professional expertise is necessary . . .' (page 81).

It takes a long time to recover from a badly executed project.

Chapter 12

The Way Ahead

An analysis of the progress of the stewardship movement over the last twenty-five years indicates that besides the very mixed reception in the early days the activity was very patchy. Some dioceses moved ahead with enthusiasm to confront the pretty solid wall of indifference and prejudice. Others took little or no action, allowing the idea to catch up with them eventually. The impact of inflation and the reduction of contributions from the Church Commissioners have forced even the most reluctant to face the necessity of finding money to balance the budget.

This has not always been to the advantage of Christian stewardship, considered by some to be entangled with theological jargon obscuring the need for quick results in the raising of money. Treating the Church as a charity and appealing for funds on the grounds that it is a good cause has not proved honouring to God, and the constant pressure upon people to meet the needs of the institution has had a debilitating effect. Where the emphasis has been on the concept of expressing commitment to the cause of Christ, and the continuing interest by God in all that he has lent to his people, there attitudes have been changed and parishes have embarked on the rising graph of parochial income and missionary giving.

The parish comes alive
Arising from reports from the dioceses, and from professional consultants, there are examples greatly to encourage others.

When attitudes are right, gratitude becomes firmly linked with generosity and fellowship begins to grow. The parish comes alive in ways that the leadership has longed for and worked for over long periods. People meet together, study and pray together. They become aware of what needs to be done; aware of those who need personal care; aware of the importance of their own pilgrimage and journey into holiness. Theoretical talk of family takes on the shape of reality as people discover each other. We avoid talking of success but we can talk of blessing as God honours those who put him first.

It would appear that the percentage of parishes which have taken stewardship seriously is very low, and that is despite the strong lead given by bishops in recent years. There is still ample room for a co-ordinated teaching programme in the Church, and we could learn from the experience in other provinces of the Anglican Communion where there is a close liaison between education, mission and stewardship. Great encouragement has been experienced when a whole diocese is able to move together. Perhaps our English dioceses are too large for this to be a practical proposition, but the signs are that some deaneries are prepared to discover themselves in a co-operative effort involving each of the parishes. This requires a courageous lead from the rural or area dean and some loss of an elusive sovereignty on the part of the constituent parishes. The gains are enormous in the lowering of barriers caused by boundaries and churchmanship. The training can be a corporate exercise, thus saving manpower and money. Help can be available from the strong to the weak without any loss of face. Financially, the whole area is released from inherited anxieties at the same time and eyes are lifted beyond parish boundaries to the demands of a much wider area. If there is to be the progress for the stewardship movement which the present situation demands, a long-term strategy must be developed. The great enthusiasm for covenants tends to limit the forward look to a calculated number of years. The Church should be free from any such restraint. Any limited period agreed for administrative purposes should be seen as steps forward on a long path. If stewardship of resources is to become a normal part of parish life the term must be unlimited. Infinity is a good concept for a Christian body to embrace. Into this can be fitted any lesser division, be it a four or seven year covenant, or the periodic examination of basic theology, or to update method.

Vision and hard work

The most important factor is a positive attitude, and this springs from a clear vision of the calling of individuals and the Church to fulfil the will of God. It is difficult to revive a fading vision in isolated units, but easier to revive it and to maintain it when enthusiasm is injected from a variety of sources. That is why a programme of deanery projects could alter the whole financial feeling in a diocese. Enthusiasm must be backed by hard work. Stewardship is no magic word offering a panacea for every parochial ill. The quickest way to discover its emptiness is to embark on a project in a half-hearted way, leaving the donkey work to 'someone else'—that mythical entity. Hard work supported by hard thinking and patient determination will produce a long term strategy for church life which will not peter out at the first interregnum or when a churchwarden retires. True vision will stimulate motivation so that worship, service and giving will measure love for God and understanding of the gospel. Thankfulness is not a temporary emotional response to a particular event, it is an ongoing attitude. Pastoral interest in, and care for, neighbour must not be spasmodic; it is strategic for the demonstration of loving care for others and cannot be left to chance. Gratitude and generosity must be linked in indissoluble union.

There is a tendency to isolate stewardship from the spiritually ordered life of a congregation in churchgoing and sacrament. In fact, in some instances the impression given is that this is less important than service and financial support. This is quite as bad as the relegation of giving as an 'unmentionable', confirming the treatment of any variety of stewardship as an optional extra. The stewardship of the life and possessions of the individual, as of the responsibilities of the whole church in obedience to Christ, is an essential response to the revelation of God. It is impossible to obey the command of Jesus to love God with the total personality and to refuse to have anything to do with stewardship. We have to start with ourselves, but there is a vast field to explore if we are to do justice to the place allocated to the human race by its creator. Every Eucharist symbolizes our creatureliness and our potential as the nourished faithful, as recipients of the benefits of the sacrifice of Christ our cross bearer and deliverance. But God's people need constantly to be reminded of the significance of our thanksgiving and it is in this area that we need our teaching sessions, either in preaching services or weekday talks or group studies. People so easily forget the divine love and action which goes before every notion of gratitude on their part. We love because he loves us.

Stewardship is not to be left as the special interest of those who feel it is important. The accusation that the needs of the church are obscured by 'too much God talk' is unworthy and reveals a terrible ignorance of what God has done in creation, redemption and in the gifts of the Spirit. Of course, Christians must be concerned for other members of the human race and must be aware of the dangers attached to a selfish exploitation of the resources of the earth. To some people ecologists are overly enthusiastic, but in sensible statements and sober action they can express something on behalf of a Christian conscience.

In these wider matters, Christian stewardship has something to say to the rest of humanity which shares with Christians a natural stewardship of body and environment. For men and women are not simply to be concerned with the well-being of their contemporaries or their successors. They must lift their eyes with the Christian in his stewardship, to God.

The way ahead for Christian stewardship must embrace humble worship, devoted service, a God honouring thankfulness and costly generosity.

The overriding consideration

No stewardship project, however satisfying and apparently successful, can ever be the end of a story. When sons and servants succumb to the temptation to believe themselves to be profitable to God and his Church, they fall into a deep and comfortable rut. Having met the challenge of stewardship, often after much travail of mind, they feel they have arrived. Released from the constraints of ecclesiastical poverty, their spiritual senses seem to begin to atrophy. They see no needs around them, for they are ever inward looking. They hear no cries of distress and pleas for aid, for they are deafened by the triumphal noises of achievement and success in their limited field of activity.

The only achievement resulting from a stewardship project which is of any value, is the clearing of the decks for action. Less important matters of consolidation and maintenance take their proper place and the church, the people of God, can get back to the business for which it was called into being, to be a mobile church with a message. The message is the gospel of God, the mission is the mission of Jesus in whose name repentance and forgiveness of sins have to be preached to all nations. St Luke spells out the dimension of the mission in the opening chapter of the Acts of the Apostles. Jesus' followers are to be his witnesses in Jerusalem, in all Judaea and Samaria and to the ends of the earth.

Witnesses for the gospel
Evangelism can never be separated from the life of the Church. It is to this end that every activity from prayer to planning must point. The Church exists for the sake of those outside its membership, and this is a reminder that a church which lives for itself will die by itself. After devotion has expressed itself in gratitude Godward, it must submit itself in worship and obedience. Not every Christian is called to be an evangelist, but each is called to be a witness. Witness does not begin and end with the individual, there can be a powerful witness from the corporate life of Christian people in attitude and action. The witness of the Society of Friends needs no long explanation.

Certain aspects of a stewardship project can lead very naturally into a programme of mission endeavour. As soon as the responsibility to be obedient in the matter of mission is taken seriously, the planning and outcome of a stewardship project can be made to further evangelistic effort. When, for instance, plans are made for a congregational meal, it is possible to have tables of such a size as to accommodate a number sufficient to form a house group. The hostess should be encouraged to invite near neighbours and friends to sit at her table not simply for this one occasion, but to be kept together for future meetings too. The house group, as it grows in mutual love and appreciation, can open its ranks to enquiring contacts with whom the good news from God may be shared.

All can minister
The Church of England has been compelled, in recent years, to take account of the reduction in the number of vocations to the ministry and to experiment in changes from the pattern of the resident priest in every parish. Non-stipendiary ministries have been established and the local ordained minister is now attracting serious consideration. At first sight this would appear to be a serious threat to the commitment of the church to be obedient to the will of God and to carry the message to 'every creature'. This would be the case if evangelism depended upon the ordained leadership alone. But the facts are that with the decline in numbers in that category there has been a greater emphasis on the real pastoral and evangelistic ministry of the lay people. There may no longer be a resident priest, but there are most probably resident Christians in every village and hamlet in the country. The ecclesiastical parishes of England have a personal Christian presence, often represented by a faithful group whose witness counts for God.

A stewardship project will have provided training for such groups, holding them together in prayer and giving them practical experience in communication as pastoral visitors, links between populace and church, people and God. As more single parishes, teams and groups, deaneries and dioceses undertake the necessary teaching and hard work involved in stewardship, so much more effective contact will be made in every community.

No one should ever be satisfied with a smoothly running

scheme which fails to take account of the need for the constant sounding of the evangelistic note through the corporate life of the congregation and the life and witness of its individual members.

Evangelism has become a jargon word with threatening overtones for the folk in the pew. It is a word used by experts and thought to be best left with them. Some think it has its beginnings with Moody and Sankey and now requires American money and expertise to be engaged in today by people who like that sort of thing. Just as a teaching programme was necessary to cleanse the word *stewardship* from the clutter of misunderstanding, so a determined effort of similar proportions must be made with the word *evangelism*. Attention will have to be drawn to the wide range of interpretation of the word in theological and organizational terms. Simplicity on the one hand and a bewildering complexity on the other are indispensable parts of the package which is not to be confined to an approach to individuals but must take account of the impact of God's offer on whole communities. Starting from a general acceptance that the Church has a mission in the world, it is necessary for church people to understand the significance of this for the non-Christian or lapsed Christian neighbours and for the community in which they live.

Each generation of Christians has to take seriously their Lord's command to preach, to teach, to heal and to deal with evil. Each generation has to involve its contemporaries in hearing and responding to the message of God. There is nothing automatic about the acceptance of the Christian faith by children of Christian parents. Each has to pay attention to the gospel and take a personal view of it. It often happens that a group of young people, who have discovered an openness in discussion in their friendship, will move together into personal faith.

Carrying the message
The establishment of a Christian stewardship project as part of

the normal life of a parish congregation presents a challenge along two lines. It must be seen, first of all, that it is not enough that the project should simply enable the church to survive. Complacency can lead so easily to apathy; freedom from stimulation can allow whole congregations to sit back in the drowsiness of self satisfaction. Secondly, an answer must be found to the question 'What shall we do next?' This sort of pressure is felt among those who have faithfully undertaken an ongoing visitation programme and, with the passage of time, see it working as a means of consolidation. They feel the urge to break out beyond the fringe to carry the gospel message to the uninitiated and uninterested. Lessons learned in the regular visitation programme, and in the experience of house groups for prayer or study, can be applied in obedience to the call to mission.

There is no prospect of response unless there is communication. St Paul quotes scripture to assure salvation to those who call upon God. Yet how shall they call upon God if they are unbelievers? How shall they believe never having heard the message? How shall they hear if there is no proclamation? There can be no proclamation without commissioned messengers. By virtue of Baptism the sons of God are one with Christ in his mission. The divine imperatives, 'Go', 'Make disciples', 'Preach', 'Teach' and 'Heal', echo down the years, addressing today's Christians with the challenge of a lifetime programme. Communication will have been a keynote in any properly mounted stewardship project. It will have been necessary for visitors to learn the art of face to face conversation, the sharing of ideas, listening to questions and expecting some reaction to the purpose of the visit. Involvement with a group for study and discussion should have taught the elements of clear statement, simple question and a restraint on the desire to be talkative. A stranger introduced to such a disciplined group would soon feel at home, not expected to say a lot yet not silenced by a dominant chairman or an ecclesiastical expert. Those who would be ambassadors for Christ must before all else be committed to serve him. They must be clear about the message they carry, and must be able to deliver it in a relevant and loving way. To this end they must study those to whom they go. There may be shared characteristics among townspeople or country folk, but there is no way of putting individual intellects and emotions into categories in order to supply some blueprint for response. The whole exercise of applying the standards of Jesus to individuals or communities must be undergirded by prayer. It is the Holy Spirit who converts. He does not destroy a character he has helped to build to make it a 'clone' of some particular kind of Christian. His spiritual gift of newness reveals the best potential of that character. We find the same phenomenon in a community whose members work with each other for the sake of their common Lord. The Christian ashram in India, the Christian co-operative, a Christian school, experiments in reconciliation in Northern Ireland all express the fellowship of the Holy Spirit.

The great commission
The Lambeth Conference of 1958 reminded the Church of the place of evangelism in the vocation and ministry of every Christian. 'Evangelism is not to be thought of as the task of a select few. Baptism and confirmation constitute "the ordination of the laity" for the task of evangelism. It is for every Christian to do what Andrew did for his brother—to say, "We have found the Messiah," and bring him to Jesus. This is the Church's prime objective.' Putting evangelism in the context of such a personal encounter as Andrew had with Peter reduces to size what for some is still a frightening prospect. Because the brothers had a real and deep relationship, they were able to communicate with each other. The personal witness of one was convincing motivation for the other to take the next step.

The history of the Church in mission is not a story of unqualified success. There have been events where missed opportunity had profound effects upon subsequent developments. Max Warren, in his book *I believe in the Great Commission* (Hodder and Stoughton, 1976), points to the consequences of what turned out to be missed opportunities.

AD 70 was a turning point in the relationship between Jews and Christians. The fall of Jerusalem to the armies of Titus was marked by the evacuation of Christians to Pella and the beginning of severance from the ancient parent religion and of centuries of bitterness. Canon Warren saw this as a dramatic failure of the Church to be true to its calling.

The bitter truth about the Church's encounter with Islam is one of abject failure too, apart from the Christ-like contribution of men like Ramon Lull who saw what a disaster were the crusades. 'It appears to me, O Lord, that the conquest of that sacred land will not be achieved . . . save by love and prayer and the shedding of tears. . .' Opportunity presented itself to Rome in the late thirteenth century, when on two occasions Kublai Khan requested missionaries, 'Send me a hundred men skilled in your religion—. . . there shall be more Christians here than in your parts.' Two Dominicans were sent; they reached Armenia and were terrified to go further.

Decline of religion

In the more recent experience of the Church in Europe since the beginning of the twentieth century, there has been an ebb tide in faith and the practices of Christian religion. Church worship has fallen off dramatically and moral standards, which were believed to be the sustaining steel of the structure of society, have been deeply eroded. Time was when two honest men could seal an agreement with a handshake; now everyone is wise to study the small print and to heed the advice, *caveat emptor*. Part of the task of preparation for evangelism is for church people to live and act as if they really believed in God. His law, his justice, his love are the regulating and healing factors of human beings' dealings with each other. 'We have found him. Come and see.' A confident assertion and a simple invitation can bring enlightenment and a reordered personality.

But our witness and our mission is not confined to our dealings with individuals as such. Even there we are powerless unless the Holy Spirit is evidently at work. God is involved in the wider canvas and has a great deal to say to the world he loves. Atheistically inclined pessimists and agnostic seekers are in these days greatly troubled by the existence of bombs and missiles stored in arsenals on both sides of the world far beyond the requirements of annihilation. It is as if the militarists, defenders of democracy, protectors of vastly stretched boundaries and keepers of the peace cannot be satisfied until provision is there for 'everyone to die twice'. It is part of our mission to heal and to deal with evil and we must declare with all the humble assurance of the faithful through the ages that Christ is Lord and powerful to act in and through his creation. He can deliver from phobias, he does support his people through stress and persecution. No one has any power, 'except it be given him from above'.

Care for the environment

Christian stewardship and human stewardship must challenge the way the earth's resources are exploited, but the Christian is as much concerned about the creator's will as the creature's comfort. Loss of nerve can only be corrected by a recovery of faith in God, the Lord of history. It is the overall dimension of God which is missing from the communications of those concerned with the protection and proper use of the earth's resources. They can see the impending disaster as it threatens the human scene and endeavour to shoulder the burden of convincing others and conserving the ecological balance in nature. The good news of God would ease the load for them and provide them with an accession of strength from the creator and preserver of mankind's environment. The Christian steward takes seriously his own responsibility for the care and management of what is another's.

None of the words which relate to God's world and his concern for the inhabitants of it confine or limit his care to a small space. His sustaining provision and divine love penetrates to all fields at all levels. A hint of this occurs at the end of the Book of Jonah, that wonderful 'cartoon of disobedience'. Jonah is given a message for Nineveh to which he objects and tries to avoid delivering. After a startling adventure, he repents, is called and sent again, proclaims a judgement and is furiously disappointed when God accepts the repentance of the city. Jonah believes that his concern for a dying plant is greater than God's love for a great city, but listens to the reminder, 'After all, it has more than six score thousand innocent persons in it, and also much cattle.' God also cares for the great number of animals.

Jonah had to be delivered from the idea that rigid dogma and unalterable proposition represent God's attitude to his creation. He had to learn that it is in the area of personal relationships that truth has a chance of emerging and change for the better can ensure. So for twentieth century people, the commitment to Christ, the practice of religion and the outward looking desire for others' well being are all of a piece. To be worthy of Christ's gospel will mean an identification with God in all his affairs, first the expansion of the government of God in human institutions, and equally the change in individuals as they respond to the call of Jesus.

Variation of gifts
The stewardship of the gospel demands that every member of the Church should discover God's special gift of the Spirit and dedicate it to be used with all the others in making the Body of Christ effective in the community. The gift of preaching and teaching is committed to those who are recognized by the Church and authorized by ordination or commission to exercise this gift in the congregation. Preaching is an essential part of evangelism, and teaching sets out the great doctrines of the faith answering the problems raised by enquiring minds. Preaching is more than the utterance of words, personality engages personality in the presence of the risen Christ and does so in mind, emotion and action. It is a God-controlled activity and often the preacher finds it difficult to recall exactly what he said which produced a response in a hearer.

Every Christian knows that he has a duty to worship God, but he is not always aware that worship can have a profoundly moving impact upon someone on the fringe of things, looking for a way home to God. The atmosphere of true worship, which avoids superficiality and a childish familiarity, can lift a seeking spirit into the high realms of contemplation, given reverence and some opportunity to be quiet.

Some congregations have found the sharing of the Peace a natural way of expressing fellowship without embarrassing the stranger, others accept the Peace as a formal part of the liturgy and use an opportunity at the end of the service to spend some time greeting each other and welcoming the newcomers. We do well to heed St Paul's exhortation, 'Let all things be done decently and in order'. There must be nothing slipshod about the ordering of the service, the choice and rendering of the music, the relevance and tunefulness of congregational hymns, thoughtful and appropriate prayers, with the occasional moments of silence when nobody does anything but wait upon God. If there is an interlude with orchestra, or guitars, or sacred dance, let these be worshipful of God and not a demonstration of human prowess—but that, of course, applies to everything.

The atmosphere of friendship

Fellowship does not evaporate at the close of Sunday worship. It is through the place of the Holy Spirit in the relationships of human friends which makes the 'friendly atmosphere' attractive to those who look on and may be moved to look in. It is the realm of fellowship that there has been the greatest progress in ecumenical endeavour; throughout the land Christians are recognizing each other as friends. Meeting, praying and sharing they present a new and winsome face to a divided and anxious world. Religious communities have always demonstrated the characteristic loving kindness of their Lord in their hospitality and service, and now there are the newer phenomena of secular communities and extended Christian families to provide a fellowship atmosphere which in itself has a converting influence. The communities in Northern Ireland are motivated by a desire to lead towards the reconciliation of an estranged and divided populace. Lee Abbey and Scargill exist for the encouragement of Christians to become effective in their witness, and by their own community life to provide the welcoming milieu in which new Christians may come to life.

It is God who is active in these manifestations of Christian endeavour. Years ago J. B. Phillips reminded us that our God is too small. Christians seem happier with limited horizons and this has the effect of inhibiting a vision which would break out of parish boundaries and open prayer beyond the selfishness of:

> God bless me
> and my wife
> Our Joe and
> his wife
> Us four, no more.

'We do not lose heart'

The gospel is for the whole world and for the whole person too, not limited to intellect, emotion or experience. St Paul knew this and encouraged a minority Church to see itself as the instrument of God in a largely hostile world. Hostility still exists, and many of our fellow Christians in various parts of the world have felt in their communities and in their own bodies the devastating effect of persecution. In Europe and America the hostility is muted, but apathy and indifference depress the Christian effort to support and further the mission of Jesus. Nevertheless the Church has many growing points, opportunities are made and others seized to share the good news of God and his kingdom. The high moments of other families' experiences invite the sympathetic friendship of Christian friends, rejoicing in birth, Baptism and marriage; supporting the bewildered bereaved with real understanding and a Christian faith.

But it is not simply on these very human occasions that contact for Christ can be made. We must not assume, either, that it is only to a person in his weakness and need that the gospel may be applied. One of the important lessons of stewardship teaching is that man may be approached in areas of his strength. Thinking again about the blessings of life, counting them, pondering some of them as undeserved miracles opens a

man's mind to measure the supposed strength of his own arm
and to look beyond himself to a little known or recognized
providence. To thank God in simple gratitude may be a first big
step in turning life into a pilgrimage.

Maintaining the evangelistic activity in obedience to the
great commission means that any suggestion that it is the
money we are after is shown up for hollow cynicism. Christ
beckons us to follow him and to become 'fishers of men', using
the large net which is not selective in its encompassing but
gathers in weak and strong, rich and poor, individuals and
groups, young and old.

Earlier it was asserted that Christian stewardship should
become part of the normal and ongoing work of the local
church. This is true and will reach its maximum usefulness if
there is a constant review of the ongoing work of the Church.
Good stewardship enables the people of God to accept their
responsibilities for kingdom extension at home and abroad.
This responsibility reaches beyond any financial commitment
to personal involvement in evangelistic prayer and effort. It is
not possible to calculate the far-reaching results in the lives of
others which spring from the obvious caring fellowship of the
Christian group. The stranger meeting with such a group
quickly assesses its warmth and atmosphere and can feel at
home in it. Cold formality which is concerned only for the
continuance of things 'as we like them' repels the potential
adherent who will bring new life, and moves into decline, giving
no evidence of the fruit of the Spirit.

Learning from Jesus

Much work has still to be done to convince many of the folk in
the pews that evangelism and witness are essential activities of
the Church and its members if they are to be loyal to the
precepts of Jesus. There are many indications in the Bible of
this essential part of the Church's work in the world. In St
Luke's Gospel there are three stages of proclamation
demonstrated by Jesus as he taught his disciples how to
communicate the message. First of all in Luke, chapter 8 verse

1, he preaches as he travels through towns and villages showing his company of the twelve disciples and the women how to meet people's need to know, how to deal with their diseases and how to confront evil. In this section there are typical parable stories which disclose his method of discourse. Moving on to Chapter 9, again at verse 1 the next stage of the training involves the despatch of the twelve disciples on their own, but with divine authority to perform the same ministry and with clear instructions about equipment and conduct. Then in Chapter 10, verse 1, the mission is opened up to a wider company of seventy-two who are commissioned to operate in pairs carrying the same message and exercising the same delegated authority. The context sounds a note of urgency and ties in the response to kingdom news with judgement, and concludes, 'whoever listens to you listens to me; whoever rejects you rejects me; and whoever rejects me rejects the one who sent me'.

This sense of urgency must return if the Church is to be effective in making new Christians. Modern man is not greatly concerned with a salvation theology which relates only to the soul's condition after death, but he has absorbed a great deal of the compassion which flows from the spirit and personality of Jesus. Urgency for him is to rescue the needy from the dominion and consequences of sin, which spoils, separates and destroys. Urgency is required to deal with the sicknesses, anxieties, phobias and psychoses of society's less than robust members. Urgency to face the strong man with the standards of Jesus and to guide him into a God-honouring pattern of life. Urgency to proclaim the story of God's love and intervention, in the coming of Jesus into human life, and to find meaning in the mystery of his death and resurrection. Forgiveness, acceptance and reconciliation bring the wanderer home and give a new intensity to his living—a here and now salvation which takes care of the hereafter.

Mission in many forms
Some churches have found benefit in mounting a teaching programme either for novices or for the encouragement to

growth in Christian living. The parish mission or the teaching mission have their place if they are related to the priorities of the church. They concentrate the normal work into a short intensive period, and give people the opportunity to survey a broad canvas in a limited period and to move to some decisive conclusion about their faith and their future. No effort of this kind should be a 'flash in the pan', with folk longing for its end that things may get back to normal! The quiet work in Sunday school, youth groups, interest groups, meetings for prayer and study and in confirmation classes must go on, for it is in these areas of Christian fellowship that witness bears fruit and the evangelistic work of the Church produces results.

Jesus referring to his death said, 'I, being lifted up from the earth will draw everyone to myself'. Thus the cross becomes the heart of the proclamation as well as the sign of identification of the Church with the purpose of God. It declares God's universal love and assures the effectiveness of Christ-centred witness. Whether as stewards, sons, servants, slaves or friends, the overall aim must be to see that the 'lifting up' is proclaimed and its benefits shared.

Our stewardship is not the end of endeavour; it beckons us forward to share what we know of the unsearchable riches of Christ with anyone whom Christ is drawing to himself.

The need for action

So we come to the end of the book with perhaps many questions unanswered. Do not leave it there; go on asking until the answers are forthcoming. One of the best ways forward is the decision for action which, accepting the human and biblical challenge to the stewardship of life, influence and resources, is prepared to launch out with others on a programme of teaching and challenge. Your experience of stewardship may date back to the very early days when a short sharp campaign produced a surprising result in finance but left a divided parish. Another may remember how soon the impact of a campaign faded when nothing further was done in subsequent years. Now is the time to begin again, with a clearer understanding of what is involved and a determination to make stewardship a part of the normal life of a parish, for its fellowship and for its individual members.

Others will recognize the source of new life and commitment and will be ever alert to maintain and extend the work of God through a proper use of resources. Even in the parishes most deeply committed to the stewardship way there is a long way ahead to worthy living. The average promise represents a lower level of devotion to God and his cause than would be expected from well taught, practising Christians. The challenge to the individual must not be blunted by their vicarious share in some imaginative community scheme run by the Church. We sing about the amazing love of Christ demanding life, soul, all. That is not the place to stop,

> 'Love so amazing, so divine
> *Shall have* my life, my soul, my all.'

Be encouraged to go with God, fired by the message of Christ's gospel, to awaken gratitude and to have it matched by generosity.

Appendix 1

SUGGESTIONS FOR BIBLE STUDIES

ON SONSHIP

THE BASIS OF ALL SOUND
STEWARDSHIP TEACHING

A. *Jesus as Son of God*

Study 1	Luke 1. 32, 35	The promise
	Luke 3. 22	Acknowledgement
	Luke 4. 3,9	Status challenged
	John 1. 34	Testimony of John Baptist
	John 3. 16	God's great gift
Study 2	John 3. 18	Challenge to belief
	John 3. 35, 36 and	Delegated power and source
	John 6. 40	of life
	John 5. 22, 23	Delegated judgement
	John 14. 13	Jesus' continuing interest
	John 17. 1	Relationship in prayer
	John 19. 7	The unbelieving crowd

B. *Disciples as sons*

Study 3	John 20. 17	The link verse
	Phil. 2. 15	God's perfect children
	1 John 3. 1, 2	God's love for his children
	Gal. 3. 26	Faith the way to sonship
	Gal. 4. 5–7	Delivered into sonship
Study 4	Heb. 2. 10	Jesus leads to glory
	Rom. 8. 14–17	Spirit and sonship
	Eph. 1. 5	Made sons because of Jesus
	Rom. 8. 31–39	The privilege of sons
	John 15. 14–17	Sons are not slaves but friends

ON MONEY   THE CARE AND DISPOSAL OF
WHICH BECOMES A MEASURE
OF RESPONSE TO THE GOSPEL

C. *An emerging pattern*
Study 5   Exod. 30. 11–17   Tax for the tent
         1 Sam. 8. 3   Pitfalls for money makers
         2 Sam. 24. 18–25   Personal cost of sacrifice
         2 Kings 12. 4–16   Temple collections
         (cf 2 Kings 22. 3–10)
         2 Kings 15. 20   Tribute taxes

D. *From the Gospel records*
Study 6   Matt. 6. 24   Which master?
         Matt. 19. 21   Money—an encumbrance?
         Matt. 27. 6–8   Tainted but used
         Matt. 28. 12–15   Bribery
         Mark. 12. 13–17   Tribute money
         Mark. 12. 41–44   Widow's offering
         Luke 3. 11–14   Tax collectors and soldiers
         John 12. 1–7   She gave. He helped himself
Study 7   Matt. 20. 1–15   Workers' wages
         Matt. 25. 14–30   Three servants
         Luke 16. 1–15   Shrewd manager

E. *Acts of the Apostles*
Study 8   Acts 2. 44, 45 and   Distribution according to
         Acts 4. 32–37   need
         Acts 5. 1–10   'The money was yours'
         Acts 8. 18–24   Salvation not for sale
         Acts 11. 27–30   The collection
         Acts 20. 31–35   Giving and receiving

F. *The Epistles*
Study 9   Rom. 15. 25–28   Reference to the collection
         1 Cor. 16. 1–4   Helping the needy
         2 Cor. 8. 1–15   Christian giving

Study 10 2 Cor. 9. 1–15   Rights and duties
           2 Cor. 12. 14   You—not your money
           1 Tim. 3. 1–7   Not to love money
           1 Tim. 3. 8   Not greedy for money
           1 Tim. 6. 10   Source of evil
           Titus 1. 11   Reprobates
           Heb. 13. 5–6   Be satisfied.

FURTHER BIBLE STUDIES WITH NOTES AND QUESTIONS

Study 11 PERSONAL RESPONSIBILITY

St Luke 12. 42: 'Who is the trusty and sensible man whom the Master will appoint as his steward . . . ?'

1 Cor. 4. 2   'Stewards are expected to show themselves trustworthy.'

1 Tim. 6. 7   'We brought nothing into the world . . .'

(a) The facts about God affect the position, function and relationship of mankind.

God is creator: Man is creature, dependent yet able to co-operate.

God is redeemer: The doctrine of the person and work of Jesus Christ affects man's effectiveness, fulfilment and destiny.

God is Spirit: The doctrine of the Holy Spirit, remembrancer, guide, enabler, impinges upon man's daily life of service and relationship.

(b) We come into the world with nothing. Everything is provided but has to be worked for. The baby is part of its parents' responsibility. Growth and maturity come from the acceptance of responsibility in ever widening circles. Without an awareness of others and their needs man exploits his environment for his own enjoyment. Without an awareness of God, he does this as part of the so called 'struggle for existence'.

(c) What would you consider to be adequate terms of reference for the task of being a faithful steward of God's provision?

    (i) In relation to God as master?
    (ii) In relation to other people?
    (iii) In relation to nature and natural resources?
    (iv) In his handling of his own personality, influence and possessions?

Study 12   AREAS OF PERSONAL RESPONSIBILITY
St Luke 10. 29–37   The parable of the good Samaritan
St Matthew 25. 14–30 The parable of the talents

(a) Ignoring priest and Levite let us concentrate on the Samaritan:

    (i) He had no natural affection for the injured man.
    (ii) It was need that appealed to his sense of responsibility.
    (iii) The need was specific and demanded immediate, definite and once for all action.
    (iv) Having decided to help he held nothing back:

        (1) his attention,
        (2) his time,
        (3) his 'first-aid' of oil and wine and bandages,
        (4) his own beast for transport,
        (5) his money,
        (6) his credit.

(b) The stewards in the talent parable are employed 'according to their capacity'. So there is not one standard of productivity; all are different but all are expected to treat the opportunities within their capacity with equal seriousness and devotion. It would have been equally possible for the man with one talent to produce two as for the man with five to fail to produce anything. Sometimes the less endowed are the most faithful.

(c) What are the areas in which a person has recognizable responsibilities? They would fall into two categories, personal and community; but could range from influence to the exercise of power and would include possessions however small.

Study 13 WHAT ABOUT MONEY

Deuteronomy 8. 17   'Nor must you say to yourselves "My own strength and energy have gained me this wealth", but remember the Lord your God.'

Jesus in Mark 10. 23 'How hard it will be for the wealthy to enter the kingdom of God.'

1 Timothy 6. 10   'The love of money is the root of all evil things.'

2 Cor 8. 1–2   'The Macedonians from the depths of their poverty have shown themselves lavishly open handed.'

(a) Money shows up people's attitudes. Riches are not dangerous in themselves, it is how they are handled that matters. It is the love of money, not money itself, which is at the root of evil. Riches as an end in themselves, or as a means of personal aggrandizement whether possessed, hoped for, schemed for, or worked for, are a soul-destroying snare. Few people really believe this for themselves.

They are convinced that an exchange with a Paul Getty would bring personal fulfilment and much benefit to needy friends! Money, as all possessions, must be made to serve the highest end of man and their use to bring glory to God.

(b) Would you agree that giving things away brings joy and personal satisfaction, particularly if it is done with love? Does this mean that part of the creator's plan for the creature is that there should be this aspect of likeness also, that as God is a giver, so man should be as well? Those who never give, who always hoard to themselves, lose their reason for living.

(c) It seems that money and anything 'possessed' is dangerous. How can we become insulated from the danger? Mary Magdalene gave the whole box of ointment. Jesus went beyond the limit of love to death in his detachment from things and his giving for others.

The Jews were reminded of the need to give in gratitude and accepted the joyful burden of the tenth before giving alms to the needy.

What is the Christian's standard of giving? It ought to witness to a real devotion to Jesus and cannot then be left to chance and the special occasion. The tenth could be a starting point for thought and prayer, allocating £100 in every £1,000 from the top of the pile for the service of God and for general benevolence. For some this proportion is right, for a few it is too little, for many it may be impossibly large. But for everyone this starting point can lead to a standard of giving by which the gift is something of which the giver is neither proud nor ashamed.

(d) The thoughtful disposal of a proportion which is a measure of devotion to Jesus, has the effect of sanctifying the whole so that none is squandered or misused.

Study 14   THE CHRISTIAN IN THE WORLD

St Luke 10. 37   'Go and do as he did.'
St Matthew 25. 40 'Anything you did for one of my brothers here, however humble, you did for me.'
St Matthew 4. 4   'Man cannot live on bread alone; he lives on every word that God utters.'

(a) There has sometimes been confusion over the place which evangelism and social responsibility have in the Christian obedience. There ought to be an acceptance of responsibility for both; neither is completely effective if it takes no account of the other. Canon Taylor said in 1968: 'If we persist in maintaining this "either/or", the things we say on both sides will sound more and more hollow. We must face the

issue and think it through to a synthesis, not a compromise.'
Obedience to the twofold commandment ought to drive us in
this 'both/and' direction.

(b) The Christian's responsibility may be said to move
outwards from himself; how far could it be thought to go?

(c) The following is a quotation of seven social evils. What
action could the Christian individual and the Christian community take against them?

 (i)   Politics without principles
 (ii) Wealth without work
(iii) Pleasure without conscience
(iv)   Knowledge without character
 (v)   Commerce without morality
(vi)   Science without humanity
(vii) Worship without sacrifice.

(d) No dole endears the two parties to the transaction to each
other. It is only love that redeems the pain of being a poor
recipient. How can Christians share the good news of Christ's
gospel without condescension and paternalism? If man lives on
every word that God utters, he must be fed with the word. How?

Study 15   THE CHRISTIAN COMMUNITY

1 Cor. 12. 27   'You are Christ's body and each of you a limb
                or organ of it.'
1 Cor. 12. 6–7 'There are many forms of work, but all of them,
                in all men, are the work of the same God. In
                each of us the Spirit is manifested in one
                particular way for some useful purpose.'

(a) Just as the individual lives personally by the principles of
stewardship, acknowledging his master, being a faithful trustee,
and giving aid and encouragement to those who come his way,
or fall within his care, so the Christian community has to be
upward looking in worship, inward looking in self criticism and
outward looking in service.

(b) Does the Christian community, as a congregation,

joyfully acknowledge God as Lord and Father in its worship and liturgy! Is this same congregation recognizable outside the church building as a living and loving fellowship; loving each other and being corporately available in love to the rest of the community. What does this love mean in practical terms?

(c) Does the Christian community see that its resources and its money are used in accordance with stewardship principles? Would the ideal of giving away £1 for every pound spent in the parish seem to be impractical and irresponsible, or could it be accepted as an ultimate aim?

What is your percentage of annual giving to other aspects of kingdom extension particularly through missionary societies for gospel preaching and living abroad?

(d) Has your church congregation ever considered the possibility and the cost of being self supporting? Do you know by how much the diocese (i.e. other parishes) would be relieved if you were self supporting?

(e) A good exercise in corporate stewardship would be to go behind the actual resources which the PCC has to handle and to do a survey of the potential of the people in giving, and then the potential of the consequent handling of increased funds by the PCC.

Study 16   PRACTICAL APPLICATION

2 Cor. 9. 8   'It is in God's power to provide you richly with every good gift; thus you will have ample means in yourselves to meet each and every situation, with enough and to spare for every good cause'.

(a) The first practical response is to believe that God can and will provide. Such faith destroys anxiety and buoys hope, leading to a quiet confidence in the supporting power of God for every right project.

(b) The second is an agonizing appraisal of the real situation of faith, devotion, obedience and effectiveness in personal lives and in the corporate life of your parish. For the first quiet and prayer is needed, for the second, after quiet and prayer, an

openness of discussion about priorities conducted in love and
honesty.

(c) The third is the production of a parish plan which will
embody the principles of stewardship and work toward the two
ends of pastoral care for God's people and the reaching out to
share with others the riches in Christ; that new Christians may
be made.

(d) A teaching programme may be required. For this there is
help obtainable from within the organization of the dioceses.

Appendix 2

EXAMPLES OF STEWARDSHIP PROGRAMMES

1. A Stewardship Programme
PCC appoints steering group

agree programme master list	sorting out session (optional) pre-publicity for programmes
recruit visitors train visitors PCC and visitors make their pledges	prepare programme brochure
parish gathering and commissioning of visitors	brochure distributed at parish gathering
visits to all on master list inviting pledges	personal contact and brochure to all not at gathering

Thanksgiving service and
presentation of pledges
Report to PCC
Follow-up
*(Sample supplied by Liverpool—
one of four programmes.)*

2. A Mission Programme

A THREE MONTH PERIOD OF PREPARATION:

Week 1	Mission officer chosen
Week 9	The director meets for briefing
Week 10–14	Home group meetings for 4 or 5 weeks
	The agenda to examine the work of the church, to identify its strengths, weaknesses, shortcomings and to indicate resources

SUMMING UP

Week 14 or 15	The parish conference
Week 15 or 16	Mission officers' meeting

BREAK BETWEEN PREPARATION AND MISSION

THE MISSION

Week 18	Mission visitors' briefing
	Service of commissioning of visitors
Weeks 19 and 20	Visiting period
Week 20	Mission officers' meeting
Week 21	Parish reception
	Service of commitment
Week 23 (Last Sunday of Mission)	Service of thanksgiving
Week 24	Final Report to the PCC

(Sample supplied by Wakefield)

3. A Mission Programme

From three months to a year required for forward planning
Pre-mission training of visitors and study group leaders. Four
meetings each and completed before mission starts.

THE MISSION

Opening Sunday:	Commissioning Service
Weeks 1 and 2:	Invitation to first gathering and to house groups
	First gathering with slide show and talk on stewardship
Weeks 3 to 9	House groups—one night a week for 1½ hours for 4–6 weeks
	Visitors invite to parish gathering and Service of Commitment
Week 10	House group leaders report to vicar, chairman and adviser
Week 11	Parish gathering and parish supper
Week 12 (Final Sunday)	Service of Commitment

(Sample supplied by Newcastle)

4. Three Year Plan and Harvest Supper

SUNDAY	MONDAY	TUESDAY	WEDNESDAY	THURSDAY	FRIDAY	SATURDAY
September 22 Sermons	23	24	25 Meet director	26	27 Ladies committee	28
September 29 Sermons	30	October 1 Visitor training (1)	2 Visitor training (2)	3	4 Ladies committee report to programme officer	5
October 6 Harvest thanksgiving services	7 Visits	8	9 Harvest supper	10 Director leaves	11	12
1st report 9p.m.	2nd report 9p.m.	3rd report 9p.m.				

Similar pattern to be followed in second and third years.

5. Three Year Plan and Parish Dinner

SUNDAY	MONDAY	TUESDAY	WEDNESDAY	THURSDAY	FRIDAY	SATURDAY
September 22	23	24	25	26	27	28
Two Sundays before Stewardship Sunday Sermon			Meeting with director	Campaign committee (Plan brochure)	Ladies committee briefing on invitations	
September 29	30	October 1	2	3	4	5
Sunday before Stewardship Sunday Sermon	Campaign committee (plan brochure and dinner)	Visitor training (1) 8p.m.	Ladies Report by 3pm Visitor training (2) 8p.m.		Parish dinner	
October 6	7	8	9	10	11	12
Stewardship Sunday Special Preacher [i.e. one who knows]	Visits		Director's report to parish meeting 8p.m.			
Visitors 1st report 9p.m.	Visitors 2nd report 9p.m.	Visitors 3rd report 9p.m.				

Similar pattern to be followed in second and third years.

6. Thanksgiving with Pastoral Link

BASIC STAGE

SUNDAY	MONDAY	TUESDAY	WEDNESDAY	THURSDAY	FRIDAY	SATURDAY
March 3rd Sermon in series of 5			28 Director arrives office established. Project committee meeting 8p.m.	29	30 Visitors' briefing meeting (1)	31
April 1 4th Sermon in series of 5 Project committe meeting p.m. or evening	2 Visitors' briefing meeting (2) 8p.m.	3	4 Visitors deliver invitations to their five families	5	6 Visitors' report meeting and Thanksgiving day briefing meeting 8p.m. (3)	7

	8	9	10	11	12	13	14
April	Thanksgiving Sunday 5th Sermon in series on Christian giving. Short meeting for visitors after service	Project committee meeting. Pastoral link planning 8p.m.	Visitors' pastoral link briefing mtg (4) 8p.m. Director departs				

	13	14	15	16	17	18	19
April	Commissioning of pastoral link visitors	delivery of first pastoral link leaflet by visitors to their five families					

Thereafter a quarterly visitation with a pastoral link leaflet prepared by project committee.

(Supplied by: The Anglican Stewardship Association, 23 Westgate Street, Bury St Edmunds, Suffolk IP33 1QG)

7. Pastoral Link Programme and Harvest Supper

SUNDAY	MONDAY	TUESDAY	WEDNESDAY	THURSDAY	FRIDAY	SATURDAY
September 22	23	24	25 Director arrives office set up Project Committee meeting 7.30p.m.	26 Visitors' briefing meeting 7.30p.m.	27	28
Pen-ultimate Sermons	Visitors' invitation briefing meeting 7.30p.m.				'If' exercise	
September 29	30	October 1	2	3	4 Visitors' report meeting and thanksgiving day briefing 7.30p.m.	5
Ultimate Sermons		Visitors deliver the invitations to their five families				

October 6	7	8	9	10	11	12
Thanksgiving Sunday Special addresses	Project Committee meeting pastoral link planning 7.30p.m.	Visitors' pastoral link briefing meeting 7.30p.m.	Harvest supper (Result shared)	Director departs		
October 13	14	15	16	17	18	19
Commissioning of pastoral link visitors	delivery of first post-campaign leaflet by visitors to their five families					

(Contributed by the author based on the A.S.A. programme)

8. A Seven Week Programme for a Stewardship Mission

First month (October)

third Sunday (16th)	Distribution of letter introducing mission together with prayer card.
fourth Sunday (23rd) 3p.m.	Afternoon training meeting for visitors.
following Friday (28th)	Distribution of literature to visitors.
fifth Sunday (30th) 10.30 a.m.	Commissioning of visitors.
following day (31st)	Visitors start first visits

    (a) to invite to house meetings

    (b) to hand over agenda for house meetings

    (c) to hand over cards for time and abilities and for financial promise.

Second month (November)

second Wednesday (9th)	Visitors complete first visit.
third Tuesday (15th) 8p.m.	House meetings by invitation to selected meeting places.
third Wednesday (16th) 4p.m.	ditto
8p.m.	ditto
third Thursday (17th) 4p.m.	ditto
8p.m.	ditto
third Friday (18th) 8p.m.	ditto

next Monday (21st)   Visitors start second visits

    (a) to invite to Thanksgiving Service and Parish Gathering

    (b) to collect the two completed cards

    (c) to help families who have not completed cards.

Third month (December)

  first Friday (2nd)   Visitors complete second visits.

  first Sunday (4th)   11 a.m. Service of Thanksgiving.

                                   12.30 Parish Gathering

(Supplied by Canterbury Diocese)

A Programme for a Weekend Workshop on Stewardship

Saturday	10.00	Assemble. Coffee.
	10.30	Introduction
	10.45	A theology of stewardship for the parish
	11.45	Parish planning
	13.15	Lunch
	14.30	The mission programme
	15.30	Composition and role of steering committee
	16.30	Tea
	17.00	Recruitment, briefing and commissioning of visitors
	17.45	Use of house groups or hall meetings
	19.00	Supper
	20.00	Mission leaflet and other literature
	21.30	Compline
Sunday	8.00	Holy Communion
	8.45	Breakfast
	9.45	Continuation and renewal
	10.30	Coffee
	10.45	Practical considerations by parish representatives
	11.45	Questions and general discussion
	13.00	Lunch

(Supplied by Canterbury diocese)

Appendix 3

THREE SHORT ROLE PLAYS

PASTORAL LINK VISITING

1. *The Brisk Visitor*
2. *Holy Joe, or the terror that flies by night*
3. *Any Questions?—or Ask and ye shall receive*

by Jim Wheldon
Lay Chairman, Parish of Upton-by-Chester

(The Anglican Stewardship Association)

1. The Brisk Visitor

Husband and wife seated. Knock at door. Husband answers (miming door opening). Visitor leaps in, brightly, almost overturning husband . . .

V.	Hello there! Here I am again! Your pastoral link visitor, no less! Well, folks, hope all is well with you and yours, and you know . . .
H.	But, may I . . . ?
V.	Now then, don't forget to be at our Christmas services, most imp . . .
W.	Perhaps I'd better . . .
V.	No, not now! I have to dash. Got badminton at 7.30! OK now, got it? Christmas services same as last year. Then home to a nice bit of pork, eh?
H. & W.	Can we just say . . .
V.	. . . and the wife wants the car for her . . . what's it? Arab Homeland Rally.
W.	I'm sure you . . .
V.	No, no! I'll see myself out. Bye bye. Happy Christmas to you all! See you all at Matins . . . (exit). (*pause*)
H.	I wonder what he wanted? Could he be from the Social Democrats?
W.	I don't know. Pity he took away the leaflet he kept waving at us. But I've seen him before somewhere.
H.	I think he may be something to do with the parish church, so he probably had the wrong house—he wanted the Jones's next door I'm sure. I'll mention it to the Rabbi when we go to tomorrow's Synagogue service, he may know something about it.

Production note: The visitor should be ten times larger than life. The sort of chap out to help the vicar whom he considers to be a 'sound chap' etc., etc. Husband and wife are cut off in their remarks, so should say, e.g. 'I'm sure you... mumble... mumble... mumble'. Timing is important. The briskness should not result in loss of understanding through too much speed. H. & W. could show some consternation at mention of Christmas services, pork dinners and Arab Homelands but not so much as to detract from last line.

2. Holy Joe, or The Terror that Flies by Night

Husband and wife sitting watching TV. Knock at door.

H.   There's the football pool collector. Where's the damn coupon? Ah! here. Now, that's 25p... *(counting money he opens door and proffers it)*. Visitor leaps in.

V.   Football coupon, eh! And I wonder what else?

H.   Well, Ha! Ha!, I just like to...

V.   The wicked shall perish in hell, I say the wicked shall perish in ... and *(looking round)* I see you have taken down that poster I gave you with its warning BE SURE YOUR SINS WILL FIND YOU OUT. In Church yesterday, were you?

W.   Well, we did mean to be ...

V.   The road to hell is paved with good intentions, I say the road to hell is paved with ... what I always say is beware of the treacherous stones that fall off the temple roof...

H.   *(weakly)* Yes, well, do sit down.

V.   Ichabod, Ichabod the outcasts perish. Few are chosen and I don't rate your chances very high... Be sure your sins, I say be sure your ...

H.   *(testily)* Yes, yes. We'll make an effort next week. Now if that's all for the moment...

V.   Miserable sinners, would ye now seek to flee? But mercy is at hand—see I will fall on my knees and pray for you. *(does so ostentatiously)* Yes, ye might well cry out in terror!

H.   You are kneeling on our cat.

W.   There, pussykins. Oh! dear, I think you've killed it *(hold up cat if possible)*.

V.   Yes, well, er *(dumbfounded)*... *(then brightly)*... Well, I must go on my way. Remember the glad tidings that I brought. Walk ye not in the councils of the ungodly, I say walk ye not in the... *(door bangs)*.

H.   No wonder we don't go to church—are they all like him?

w.   I don't think so. But he shouldn't have called Mummy the 'whore of Babylon' just because she changed trains at Walsingham...

H.   No, or given the kiss of life to that pretty young Mrs Brooks when she dozed off while he was talking . . .

w.   And poor pussy. What a way to go. And his offer of a second-hand Do-it-Yourself Animal Cremation Kit wasn't tactful. Hey, listen! Isn't that him next door at the Jones's? *(shouting off stage:* Throw out the lifeline! Thou shalt not suffer a witch to live! Bad cess to ye all! etc.)

Production note: Visitor is unsmiling, harsh voiced and hectoring. A good part for someone! There could be a loud meeow when the cat is knelt on, possibly by H. or W.

3. Any Questions?—or Ask and Ye shall Receive

H. Yes, dear, you are right. We should make more effort to understand our faith. I wonder if there is a Bible study group in the parish... *(knock at door)* I'll go... *(opens door)*

V. Hello, good people! Your friendly neighbourhood pastoral link visitor is here again. Sorry I missed the last two visits. Never mind, here's Jack Wittering at your service, what?

W. Oh I'm so glad. We wanted to ask you about our daughter who has married an Independent Baptist who wants her to be baptized again by total immersion... we always thought that...

V. Typical sloppy thinking, if I may say so! By-passing the central issue. What did Commander High-price say about the binmen's bonus renegotiation, eh? Answer me that!

H. We have always been Anglicans, and we want to decide responsibility in this... It's a difficult choice.

V. I'll tell you what to do. Now take this local council. It's a straight choice between Commander Highprice and Comrade Bullrush and we've got a meeting next...

W. But you said you were from the church... isn't this a religious visit?

V. It is! The church must be involved. You take Councillor Stock—not only a lying toad, a party renegade, a defector, a lickspittle but also a Methodist. The right way for us Anglicans is...

H. What about our daughter...?

W. And when is the Bible study group starting...?

H. Oh yes, where do I get a covenant form? *(pause)*

V. That's a nice clock you've got there. Let me know if you want to sell it at any time... I must be off... only got two more calls, thank goodness. How's your Uncle Charlie these days?

H.   We haven't got an Uncle Charlie.

V.   *(surprised)* Oh, are you sure? Well, Mr and Mrs Smithson . . .

H.   Our name is Roberts . . .

V.   Never mind. I'll be back in three months. Don't be afraid to ask questions. After all, how else are you going to find out? That's what pastoral link is all about!

Appendix 4

SAMPLE INVITATIONS

Invitations should be printed on firm card with space for personal details to be written in. Remember that first impressions must be good impressions. Invitations should always be delivered personally and never posted.

1. To a Parish Meal:

> The Rector and Churchwardens of
> St Mary's Parish Church
> request the pleasure of the company of
>
> ....
>
> at a Celebration Supper in the Forum Hall on
> Saturday, 28 September 1985
>
> 7.30 for 8 o'clock   RSVP to PCC
>   secretary

2. To a Thanksgiving Service:

**The Chairman and Committee of the
Thanksgiving Programme**

invite

....

to attend the Thanksgiving Service at
St Mary's Church
on Sunday, 29 September 1985
at 10.30a.m.

Remember the important details: date, time, and place.

Appendix 5

SAMPLE MENUS FOR A PARISH MEAL

Using a great number of willing helpers from the congregation to provide a meal for everyone else is not a good idea. A parish meal ought to cater for every member to have a relaxed and enjoyable evening, with service that does not involve anyone with feelings of guilt that half the folk are working.

Secondly, a meal ought to be substantial if you expect the men to turn up. A couple of dainty sandwiches on a cardboard plate with a sausage roll and a fancy cake will do little for a feeling of internal comfort and well-being, especially if there is a notice that only one glass, apple juice or cider, can be supplied!

In the winter, warm them up. In the summer, keep them cool. Kitchen facilities will have some bearing on the menu chosen.

Starters:	Soup *or* melon *or* pate with toast *or* crisp biscuits *or* grapefruit.
Main course:	A meat casserole. This can be made with the vegetables in the casserole with the meat, using 'cook-in' sauces for convenience and for flavour.
	Additional green vegetables e.g. peas.
OR	Cold ham *or* mixed cooked meats with salad, beetroot, chutney and pickles.
	Jacket potatoes *or* French bread *or* rolls and butter.
Sweet:	Fruit salad and cream *or* trifle *or* hot mince pies with cream *or* apple pie with cream.
Coffee	

Appendix 6

OUTLINE FOR AUDIO/VISUAL SLIDES AND SCRIPT

Subjects for slide presentation

1.	View across still water	*In the beginning God created*
2.	'Adam and Eve'	*Mankind – the Image and the Delegate*
3.	View of earth from the moon	*This is God's world*
4.	Aerial view of the parish	*Our little patch in God's world*
5.	The parish staff	*Full (and part-time) leadership*
6.	The youth club	
7.	Uniformed organizations	
8.	Mothers' Union	
9.	Working parties	*The parish in fellowship and service*
10.	Sporting activities	
11.	Bell ringers	
12.	Study groups	
13.	Table prepared for Holy Communion	*The family at worship*
14.	Bread and wine	*God's gifts—human labour*
15.	Harvest offerings—produce and cash	*All things come from God . . .*
16.	A person knitting	*Everyone has gifts, abilities, skills*
17.	A person working tapestry	*Women and men specialize in their hobbies*
18.	A man digging in a garden	
19.	A cabinet maker	

20. People at work
    (a) Bank manager
21. (b) Teacher
22. (c) Doctor and nurse
23. (d) Milkman
24. (e) Refuse collector
25. (f) Postman
26. (g) Telephone engineer
27. (h) Social worker
28. View of the town hall
29. View of the church
30. Picture of the largest
    congregational group
    possible

Daily work takes up most of the time and uses up most of the skill of the individual

Centre of civic activity

The sign of God's presence

Those on whom God depends

NOTES: It is important that you should have your script specially written so that it may be topical and relevant to your own parochial or town situation.

With the advent of video, the once popular slide show is being eclipsed. There are video tapes which may be hired, but it would be better to use the skills of your local amateur enthusiasts to make your own video from your own script.

Appendix 7

KEEPING RECORDS

The incumbent, as spiritual leader, and the chairman of a stewardship project as administrator, when dealing with visitors who maintain pastoral links with families, needs to have access to accurate records. As visitors are responsible for a number of families, they themselves should be members of a team with their own leader, and all the leaders must be linked with the overall conductor of the visiting programme. Many parishes have found that an index system obtainable from Messrs D. Matthews and Son of Dale Street, Liverpool, suits this need admirably. It is called the *Slotindex* and its size is most appropriate to contain all necessary information. Each panel has 35 two-inch slots, and panels can be joined to one another to provide enough slots to compass the whole visitation programme. White cards can be inserted for families to be visited; yellow cards can indicate visitors; green cards for team leaders and other colours for the chairman, and for as many vice-chairmen as he needs. Each vice-chairman would probably need six panels.

It is best for a local handyman to fix the panels to a plywood board which can be hung in a vestry and moved when necessary to serve as a guide in meetings. The plywood board should be larger than immediate need would demand so that there could be room for more sets of six panels as the scheme expands.

With a good record board every one knows the actual visitation plan and the personnel are clear about their own place in the scheme. *But it must be kept up to date.*

The record board helps to emphasize the essentially personal nature of the ongoing contact between visitor and visited, and between the various members in the team structure. Those operating the scheme depend upon each other for encouragement and support as they strive for success.

Bibliography

Christian Giving, V. S. Azariah (Lutterworth, 1954)

A Theology of Christian Stewardship, T. A. Kantonen (Fortress Press, Philadelphia, 1956)

Let's think about money, Ellis Cowling (SPCK, 1958)

What is Christian Giving? Brian Rice (SCM Press, 1958)

Stewardship in the New Testament, H. Rolston (John Knox Press, Richmond Virginia, 1959)

Money in Christian Life, Hunter Johnson (CIO, 1960)

Before His Face, Canon H. N. Hodd (CIO, 1960)

Getting and Spending (No. 8 of *Thinking Things Through*), J. Singleton (SCM, 1960)

Stewardship in Contemporary Theology, Ed. T. K. Thompson (Associated Press, New York, 1960)

Money and the Kingdom, Five Bishops (CIO, 1961)

Christian Stewardship and Ecumenical Confrontation, A report (Churches of Christ USA, 1961)

How Christian is our Stewardship? Gordon Strutt (CIO, 1962)

God and Mammon, K. F. W. Prior (Hodder & Stoughton, 1963)

God's Stewards, Helge Brattgard (Augsburg Publishing, 1963)

Handbook of Stewardship Procedures, T. K. Thompson (Prentice Hall Inc., New Jersey, 1964)

The Question of Christian Stewardship, James Mark (SCM, 1964)

Stewardship and Evangelism, Brian Rice (SPCK, 1964)

The Stewardship Call, W.J. Werning (Concordia Publishing, St Louis Missouri, 1965)

Christianity and the Affluent Society, B.K. Rice and R.H. Fuller (Hodder & Stoughton, 1966)

The Responsible Church, Ed. Edwin Baker (SPCK, 1966)

Preaching Stewardship, C. Fehrenbach (St Andrew's Press, Edinburgh, 1967)

The Christian Stewardship of Money, (CIO, 1970)

Through the eye of a needle, Derek Farrow (Epworth Press, 1979)

A Theology of Generosity, Badger Berrie (Mowbray, 1981)

Stewardship and Sharing, Phyllis Carter (Mowbray, 1981)

Money Talks, Tom Rees (Hildenboro Hall, undated)

141

Index